Praise for *The Way of Effortless Mindfulness*

"In this groundbreaking guidebook, Loch Kelly offers contemporary versions of ancient practices to help us access the fundamental experience of being aware. *The Way of Effortless Mindfulness* teaches a unique form of mindfulness, which is advanced, yet simple. Loch offers effective ways to shift from focusing on *what we are aware of*, to *awareness of awareness*, which is one component of integrating consciousness, a process that can liberate our lives with meaning, connection, and clarity. What a beautiful book!"

DANIEL J. SIEGEL, MD
author of *Aware: The Science and Practice of Presence*

"*The Way of Effortless Mindfulness* is a profound and practical book of spiritual guidance. If you are really ready to awaken through and through, read this book, put it into practice, and it will transform your life."

ADYASHANTI
author of *The Most Important Thing*

"Loch Kelly offers a rich array of unique mindful glimpses that reveal our naturally awake, openhearted awareness. His guidance is clear, precise, and arises from a wise, caring heart. There are very few who can guide with such mastery. For those dedicated to realizing what is beyond our dualistic perceptions, *The Way of Effortless Mindfulness* is truly a gift."

TARA BRACH, PHD
author of *Radical Acceptance*

"Many of us have heard that it takes years of discipline and effort to tame the mind in order to taste awakening. Loch Kelly travelled to India and Nepal to find traditions that could directly access our natural awakeness. In this profound book, he offers his contemporary ways to 'glimpse' our awake nature immediately and heal our wounded parts. When Loch and I have taught together, I have found, for myself and students, that Loch's practices are amazingly effective. *The Way of Effortless Mindfulness* brilliantly weaves together meditation, neuroscience, and psychotherapy to truly support a compassionate awakening."

RICHARD SCHWARTZ, PHD
founder of Internal Family Systems (IFS)

"*The Way of Effortless Mindfulness* is a wonderful, timely book! There is this natural ground of our consciousness which is not bound by thoughts and emotions, from which we can experience true freedom by seeing reality clearly. Such consciousness is the effortless mindfulness taught in many sacred traditions. Loch Kelly skillfully explains how we can access it. I hope many people will read this guidebook to illuminate their path of awakening."

ANAM THUBTEN
Tibetan Buddhist teacher and
author of *The Magic of Awareness*

"Loch provides, in a single work, a comprehensive guide that spans the entire spectrum of effortless mindfulness practice. Loch does this by expertly sharing meditation from a wide variety of cultures and traditions. *The Way of Effortless Mindfulness* is written from deep mastery and personal experience. You feel that as you read, and it's inspiring."

SHINZEN YOUNG
author of *The Science of Enlightenment*

"*The Way of Effortless Mindfulness* is a deep drink of water for the thirsty heart. It is a practical guide for cultivating states of ease, compassion, and creative flow, yes. It is also a celebration of our birthright. Loch Kelly reminds us that awakening does not have to hurt. We were born to take refuge in our interconnectedness with All That Is. And it is from this place of graceful presence that we have hope of stepping up to alleviate suffering around us."

MIRABAI STARR
author of *Wild Mercy*

"*The Way of Effortless Mindfulness* is a brilliant and essential meditation guidebook. Loch beautifully introduces us to the next stage of mindfulness, bringing it into heartfelt relationship with others. In Loch Kelly, you've found a wonderful guide for the important journey of awakening, which is so vital in our world today."

LAMA SURYA DAS
author of *Awakening the Buddha Within*

"Now that mindfulness is widely embraced by mainstream culture, it may be possible for greater numbers to take a deeper step into effortless mindfulness. Though there is an initial effort, Loch helps us discover an awareness that's already effortlessly awake. *The Way of Effortless Mindfulness* is an elegant, slim volume of grace that many will benefit from. May this profound guidebook help you live a compassionate, awakened life, so needed in times like ours."
TERRY PATTEN
author of *A New Republic of the Heart*

"Loch Kelly presents a groundbreaking approach with a unique form of mindfulness—a path both gentle and powerful. *The Way of Effortless Mindfulness* makes an important contribution to our growing understanding that spiritual awakening and personal healing are two sides of the same valuable coin."
JUDITH BLACKSTONE, PHD
author of *Trauma and the Unbound Body*

"Inspiring and practical, *The Way of Effortless Mindfulness* offers us an owner's manual for awakening to our fullest potential as human beings. Through simple yet powerful exercises, Loch Kelly provides direct path teachings that exquisitely point to and allow us to easily recognize our most essential nature that lies at the heart of unbreakable well-being. This is an inspirational gem of a guidebook for accessing the spiritual wisdom that lies at the core of our humanness."
RICHARD MILLER, PHD
author of *The iRest Program
for Healing PTSD*

"*The Way of Effortless Mindfulness* is an extraordinary guidebook. With deep simplicity and subtle clarity, Loch Kelly offers us ways to glimpse the natural, ever-present awareness that is our True Nature and presents mindfulness teachings and micro-meditations that reveal it 'effortlessly' within ourselves."
KRISHNA DAS
chant leader and Grammy®-nominated vocalist

"Are you curious about the whole mindfulness thing and not sure where to start? Or are you a seasoned mindfulness practitioner who thinks they know all there is to know about this whole mindful thing? Well, Loch Kelly is your guy and *The Way of Effortless Mindfulness* is your book. Loch, in very clear and concise writing, brings so many new (or often overlooked) pointers, practices, and teachings to the table. This is an exceptionally accessible book for anyone interested in a new version of mindfulness. Oh, how I wish I had Loch Kelly's *The Way of Effortless Mindfulness* when I first began my spiritual exploration. Thank you, Loch, for knocking this one out of the park!"   CHRIS GROSSO
author of *Dead Set on Living*

"*The Way of Effortless Mindfulness* artfully challenges and guides us to make the important leap from our conditioned mind into awake, heartfelt awareness. Inspired by nondual Tibetan teachings, this original, insightful, good-humored, and psychologically savvy book opens new vistas and offers a treasure trove of illuminating practices. Welcome to awakening with small glimpses in the midst of your daily life. Highly recommended!"
JOHN PRENDERGAST, PHD
author of *In Touch*

"Loch Kelly's cutting-edge new book offers a comprehensive program of direct path practices for recognizing, abiding in, and living from our natural awake awareness. *The Way of Effortless Mindfulness* is a brilliant and original guidebook uniting "nondual mindfulness," neuroscience, and psychotherapy. It will be helpful both for newcomers and for those ready to live an embodied, awakened life. I highly recommend this book!"
STEPHAN BODIAN
author of *Beyond Mindfulness*

"I love this book because it is so practical. It contains a treasure trove of simple and effective exercises that help us to realize our true nature. Loch Kelly shows us that enlightenment is not esoteric and elusive, but always close to us, and always accessible. In *The Way of Effortless Mindfulness*, Loch shows us how to gain access to it."   STEVE TAYLOR, PHD
author of *The Leap* and *Spiritual Science*

"Once again, Loch Kelly has done a masterful job of sharing accessible, wise, and compassionate meditations and teachings. *The Way of Effortless Mindfulness* offers a doorway into a profound, cutting-edge form of mindfulness. With Loch's guidance, effortless mindfulness can become accessible to anyone. Try them out, go into them deeply, and watch these practices change your life!" DIANA WINSTON
director of mindfulness education at UCLA
and author of *The Little Book of Being*

"Loch has a deep understanding of meditation and manifests the wisdom and compassion that comes from this. In *The Way of Effortless Mindfulness*, Loch shows us how to practice a unique form of mindfulness. These effortless mindfulness practices are directly in line with the beneficial qualities of effortless awareness that my neuroscience lab has studied. I wholeheartedly recommend these practices to my students, and to you."

JUDSON BREWER, MD, PHD
director of research at Brown
University Mindfulness Center and
author of *The Craving Mind*

"Loch Kelly's book is one of the most important awakening manuals of our times. There is no doubt that *the definitive revolution* for our world is the waking up and growing up of humankind. Loch's deep heart and profound wisdom shine through the words in a way that makes awakening available to us no matter our backgrounds, belief systems, or previous experience. *The Way of Effortless Mindfulness* is a set of valuable keys to the treasure that is already within you." KURT JOHNSON, PHD
coauthor *The Coming Interspiritual Age*

The Way of
Effortless Mindfulness

Also by Loch Kelly

Books

*Shift into Freedom: The Science and Practice of Open-Hearted Awareness
(Loch's bestselling book, also available as an audiobook)*

Audio Programs

*Shift into Freedom: A Training in the Science and Practice
of Open-Hearted Awareness (audio of glimpse practices)*

*Effortless Mindfulness Now:
Awakening Our Natural Capacity for Focus, Freedom, and Joy*

The Way of
Effortless Mindfulness

A REVOLUTIONARY GUIDE
FOR LIVING AN AWAKENED LIFE

Loch Kelly

sounds true
BOULDER, COLORADO

Sounds True
Boulder, CO 80306

The exercises in this book are not intended as a substitute for medical or psychological
advice, diagnosis, or treatment. Please seek the advice of a qualified medical expert or
licensed psychotherapist first if you need treatment or care of any sort.

Published 2019

Cover design by Lisa Kerans
Book Design by Beth Skelley

Printed in the United States of America

Library of Congress Cataloging-in-Publication Data

Names: Kelly, Loch, author.
Title: The way of effortless mindfulness : a revolutionary guide for living
  an awakened life / Loch Kelly.
Description: Boulder, CO : Sounds True, 2019. | Includes bibliographical
  references and index.
Identifiers: LCCN 2018046560 (print) | LCCN 2018049998 (ebook) |
  ISBN 9781683642336 (ebook) | ISBN 9781683642329 (pbk.)
Subjects: LCSH: Mindfulness (Psychology) | Attention. | Awareness. |
  âSamatha (Buddhism)
Classification: LCC BF637.M56 (ebook) | LCC BF637.M56 K45 2019 (print) |
  DDC 158.1/3—dc23
LC record available at https://lccn.loc.gov/2018046560

10 9 8 7 6 5 4 3 2

For Tom, my father, whose death illuminated my path.
Maggi, my mother, my first teacher and inspiration,
who before she passed on, set her burdens down
and fully embraced life. And to all my teachers
and students for their love and commitment
to living an awakened and compassionate life.

Contents

Introduction

My life before I began to practice effortless mindfulness was completely different from the way it is now. Growing up, I was neither calm nor contemplative. I struggled with some form of dyslexia and ADD, and I had an underlying feeling that something wasn't quite right, that something was missing or out of balance. The only time I experienced relief from this background anxiety was while engaged in sports, feeling myself in my body and in "the zone." Once, during an ice hockey game in junior high school, the score was tied 1–1, and after the last time-out, I dropped into a sense of well-being, effortless focus, and connection with my teammates. It was as if time slowed down, and playing together in this concentrated way brought me into a profound sense of embodied joyful flow! It was after this taste of effortless mindfulness that I started wondering: *How did this happen, and could I find a way to intentionally access this joy of being in other parts of my life?*

As I grew up, I became increasingly curious about and hungry for other ways of experiencing this dimension of life. Like many in my generation, I tried reading spiritual books, traveling, romantic relationships, artistic pursuits, being in nature, and even sex, drugs, and rock and roll as I sought lasting happiness. My search eventually led me to graduate school in psychology and spirituality, where a new door opened. I received a travel fellowship to study at a university in Sri Lanka and at meditation centers in India and Nepal. There I met teachers who devoted their lives to meditation, awakening, and compassionate living. With one of these teachers, Tulku Urgyen Rinpoche, I was introduced to the advanced yet simple approach called *effortless mindfulness*, which is a different form of mindfulness from the kind that is so popular in the West today. Effortless mindfulness is a way of opening to a natural, wise, and loving awareness that is already present within us, which reveals qualities of well-being, clarity, and compassionate action. It is a way of shifting out of the chattering mind and into the source of our mind, which is already awake and aware—where we can rest, engage, and feel unconditional love. Effortless mindfulness is a unique form of mindfulness that allows us to immediately open to clarity and love in the midst of our busy everyday lives. The way of effortless mindfulness is about both waking up and growing up, so it combines a unique meditative and psychological approach to healing trauma and living an awakened life.

Effortless mindfulness gave me a way of relieving my underlying suffering and connecting to an inner joy that I didn't even know existed. My life is freer and easier than it was before I discovered effortless mindfulness, and for this I am deeply grateful. One example I can share is that writing my first book, with my dyslexia and ADD, took me ten years. Given the title of this book, *The Way of Effortless Mindfulness*, it might not surprise you that I wrote it through the practice of effortless mindfulness. Though there was still the pain of writing with ADD, this book flowed out into form in just nine months. The gift of effortless mindfulness has been finding a new willingness to show up fully with my quirks and struggles. The more I'm able to let go, the greater the unconditional, loving support that has appeared within, around, and throughout my life. I experience deeper levels of vulnerability and courage by opening to parts of myself that I avoided in the past. I've been able to feel my interconnectedness with other living beings, and as a result, I've gained a new level of motivation to be of service.

Since my first encounter with effortless mindfulness over three decades ago, developing this practice within myself and teaching it to others has been my life's inspiration and vocation. This book is meant to be like a letter to a friend. It is an invitation. I am more of a coach or a guide than a preacher or a guru. I am here to share pointers and principles so you can find effortless mindfulness for yourself, as if to say, "Hey, the water is great! Come on in! Guess what? We can awaken together!" I am convinced that accessing the natural well-being of unconditional love is learnable and teachable and hope this book will help you find what is already yours.

A Different Form of Mindfulness

Effortless mindfulness is a unique form of mindfulness. What most people in the West know as mindfulness, I call *deliberate mindfulness*. The teachings of deliberate mindfulness stem primarily from the Theravada and Zen traditions of South and East Asia and the initial practices of Tibetan Buddhism. Deliberate mindfulness has also been brought into secular settings in the United States through mindfulness practices for physical and psychological treatment and stress reduction, such as Mindfulness-Based Stress Reduction (MBSR). I love these practices because they provide a way of cultivating calm, patience, and intentional lovingkindness. I have taught deliberate mindfulness for decades as a teacher at New York Insight Meditation Center and have seen the practice help countless people. I deeply value deliberate mindfulness and its benefits. I am grateful for the popularity it is gaining in the West because it is allowing people to find greater peace of mind.

Effortless mindfulness, on the other hand, can be considered a different form of mindfulness, which is sometimes taught after having developed a deliberate mindfulness practice. It can also be a helpful alternative approach for those who have had difficulty with concentration practices or sitting meditation. Though often considered advanced, it can be a good starting place for people who are new to meditation. The effortless mindfulness practice begins with an opening to an already awake, optimal mind from which we can be effortlessly focused. The full unfolding leads to a life that is not more detached, however, but more embodied, intimate, courageous, and wise.

Effortless mindfulness has its roots in the world's wisdom traditions that are often described as *direct path, essence traditions,* or *nondual traditions.* The premise of the direct approach in all meditative traditions is that *the awake loving nature we are seeking is already here within us and can be accessed immediately.* The primary nondual tradition that the effortless mindfulness map and practices in this book draw from is called Sutra Mahamudra, which began in North India and links the three main traditions of Buddhism: Theravada, Mahayana, and Tibetan. Sutra Mahamudra was primarily a movement of lay practitioners who developed a style of practice to facilitate awakening—a shift and upgrade of awareness, mind, and identity—in the midst of everyday life. Effortless mindfulness is ideal for our contemporary Western culture in that it demonstrates that awakening is possible for anyone without having to leave home, friends, work, or family.

Benefits of Effortless Mindfulness

In bringing effortless mindfulness into the contemporary Western context, I have grown increasingly interested in the particular obstacles and supports to living a genuine, awakened life. In this book, I present a way of working with the emotional, energetic, and psychological aspects of our human experience and identity. However, this book isn't about the philosophy of consciousness, mindfulness, or awakening. I present a theory and hypothesis, but also a set of practices so that you can experience the results for yourself. I have included plenty of meditations that are direct and experiential—glimpses into a whole new way of seeing and being. With effortless mindfulness, you'll uncover a sense of well-being that relieves suffering at its root.

Students who consistently practice effortless mindfulness describe a relief from judgmental thinking, a deep sense of safety and well-being, a sense of openness and interconnection, and an ability to welcome strong emotions with less worry, fear, and shame. They also experience more compassion for themselves and others; a greater motivation, clarity, and optimal functioning at work; and a new capacity for creativity and loving relationships.

I believe that no matter where you are on your life's journey or in your meditation practice, you'll find something of benefit in engaging effortless mindfulness. I am convinced, after decades of studying, practicing, seeing students' progress, and conversing with colleagues, that awakening is truly possible in the midst of our everyday lives. This is possible because the awake nature that we are seeking is already here and available within us. Awakening is part of our common human heritage, spanning all traditions and cultures. In fact, I see clear indications that awakening is the next natural stage of human development. I have seen how those who are awakening have naturally begun to heal, teach, and support others, which seems to be part of a consciousness revolution.

Many of us are concerned about social, political, economic, and environmental issues on this planet. I believe that taking responsibility to find our own true sense of compassionate interconnectedness, and then helping others do the same, can be a radical collective healing that can bring a better future for all of us. My intention with this book is to bring a particular approach to awakening into our world so that it can transform our lives and communities.

The Flow and Structure of This Book

The Way of Effortless Mindfulness is a unique, comprehensive guidebook to an advanced yet simple form of mindfulness that brings immediate and lasting benefits. It offers a systematic map to navigate consciousness. I begin by introducing ways of discovering an already awake awareness that is the source of your mind and identity through experimenting with micro-meditations or "mindful glimpses" and noticing the results. Each individual will find that different glimpses are more suited to them than others, and the unfolding is equally unique.

Part 1 of the book starts by introducing the fundamentals of effortless mindfulness. Then I compare and contrast effortless mindfulness with the more familiar deliberate mindfulness in order to give you a clear sense of this lesser-known style. I go on to introduce the Five Foundations of Effortless Mindfulness and a series of practices that are effortless-mindfulness versions of classical deliberate-mindfulness practices such as one-pointed focus, lovingkindness, and insight meditation.

Part 2 is a deeper dive into effortless mindfulness as a way of living an awakened life. Here I point to details of the map of awakening and give a series of mindful glimpses for each of the Five Foundations of Effortless Mindfulness. I am interested in offering a set of practices for effortless mindfulness just as there are standard deliberate-mindfulness practices. Some of my standard mindful glimpses are also available in my first book, *Shift into Freedom*, and in audio and video form, so you can listen to them after you read them.

Part 3 offers ways of further supporting awakening, along with an appendix that discusses some of the traps and detours that prevent us from unfolding and embodying awakening. I describe the integration of awakening and psychotherapy and conclude with tools and techniques to continue your journey of embodying effortless mindfulness.

This is a practice book to help you not only understand effortless mindfulness, but most importantly, to experience it and embody it—to live from effortless mindfulness. If you had picked up a book about how to ride a bicycle, intellectual explanations would not be the primary way to learn, and the same applies here. Instead, I encourage you to adopt a beginner's mind, open your heart, and enjoy the ride.

Part I
Discovering

1

The Next Stage of Mindfulness

Most of us love the feeling of effortlessness. Some of the happiest times in our lives happen when we flow with the silent music of life. The sight of a dancer, athlete, or bird moving with ease and grace inspires us. What if you could learn to shift into a level of mind in which suffering could be relieved and wisdom, love, and joy naturally uncovered? What if you could discover a reliable way to access a sense of safety and open-heartedness that shifts us out of the confusion we have been so tightly caught in? What if awakening—shifting your consciousness into a more compassionate way of seeing and being—were something you could learn? What if there were an art, a science, and even repeatable methods to live from effortless mindfulness? My experience is that there are! This reality has been reported by ancient wisdom traditions and by many people I've met, and it's possible for you.

Effortless mindfulness is both a natural capacity and a skillful way to connect with ourselves and others. It is a way of being mindful from a different level of mind than we are used to. There is more to effortless mindfulness than meditation. Effortless mindfulness is primarily an off-the-meditation-cushion way of weaving together contemplation and compassionate actions. Effortless mindfulness begins by opening to a natural spacious awareness in order to become more wise, embodied, and creative. A new ethical motivation springs from the realization of a loving interconnection with all of life.

When I teach effortless mindfulness, I'm often asked, "How do I know when I'm really doing it? What does effortless mindfulness feel like?" Each person experiences a different facet of the diamond of effortless mindfulness as it shows its qualities to us freshly each time. A glimpse of effortless mindfulness might initially feel like any of the following:

- You feel relief.

- Your mind is wide open and without an agenda.

- Your thoughts are less prominent or have moved into the background.

- You are free of worry, fear, and judgment.

- You are able to effortlessly focus on something, without concentrating.

- Your center has moved from your head to your heart.

- You are resting as a field of seamless awareness that is outside and within your body.

- You feel aware from the Now and able to be aware of the past, present, or future when needed.

- Everything seems to be flowing easily, happening naturally without any effort.

- You experience a sense of joy and well-being not related to what is happening.

- You are aware from boundless, interconnected, loving presence rather than a detached point of view.

- You feel aware from nonconceptual awareness rather than thought.

- You know all is well, with nothing missing
  and nothing to push away.

Introducing Mindful Glimpses

One of my main techniques for connecting and experimenting with effortless mindfulness is through what I call *mindful glimpses.* Many people have told me that this is one of the simplest, most elegant, and effective ways to learn effortless mindfulness. A glimpse is a type of shifting, letting go, dropping, or stopping to allow a natural clarity and connectedness to emerge. Glimpses are the initial effortless effort of opening, surrendering, resting, or turning awareness around to find our open mind and open heart. They are "micro-meditations" or "rest stops" where we can refresh or reboot our whole body-mind system. A glimpse is not an insight from our conceptual mind; it is the direct experience of the essential peace, love, and wisdom that's always been here. It is a paradigm shift, an identity shift, a shift of consciousness to a new view and a new you that feels true. In Tibetan Buddhism, glimpsing is sometimes called "flashing on awakened heart-mind."

A mindful glimpse is similar to a Zen *koan,* a simple inquiry that can't be solved through logic and that takes you out of your conceptual mind and small self. Unlike a koan, a glimpse does not start with thinking. It starts with awareness unhooking from thought. The effortless mindfulness glimpses I offer in this book can be done with eyes closed or open anytime during your day. They initially take from ten seconds to ten minutes to do, but they shift you into a new operating system that allows you to enjoy their continuous benefits. The primary way of practicing effortless mindfulness is *small glimpses, many times.*

You can see glimpses as invitations to pause and shift your awareness, to have a chance to taste the peace beyond conceptual understanding. Several of my students have told me that dropping into one small glimpse has been as life changing as going on a long meditation retreat. I have found that different glimpses work well for different people depending on their learning styles. So if one glimpse in this book doesn't click for you, no worries. Just keep reading and try the next one.

When we do traditional sitting meditation, it can take a long time for the mind to settle. In contrast, here's an example to give you the direct experience of the immediacy of a glimpse.

GLIMPSE **Wordless Awareness**

1. Allow your awareness to move from reading these words to hearing the sounds around you.

2. Now shift from hearing sounds to an interest in the open, objectless space all around.

3. Rest into this alert wordless awareness. ■

After you have read the mindful glimpses in this book, I suggest you record the ones you like best in your own voice, at a pace that seems right for you, and then listen to your own voice lead you home.

You May Not Know That You Know This Already

When I describe effortless mindfulness, some people tell me they've had this feeling walking in nature, playing music, gardening, making love, driving a car, or during a special moment in their past that they long to return to. Many of us have been intuitively practicing some form of effortless mindfulness throughout our lives—while being creative, with loved ones, or while playing sports. And some of us have experienced it when we suddenly became calm and clear during a crisis.

For example, we may have shifted into effortless mindfulness while hiking with friends. While hiking, we may notice that as soon as we reach the summit of the hill, our goal seeking stops for that moment. Our identity as a seeker relaxes as we look at the sky and feel our awareness and mind open into it. We might look at our friends and feel a sense of connection and open-heartedness. We feel fully present, with no problems to solve and nothing to push away. We look at the trees and feel connected and part of nature. Our separate sense of self relaxes to reveal a wordless experience that rests in a place of "all is well." At times like these, we feel freedom, clarity of mind, joy, connection to nature and other people, and a sense of well-being. However, we often associate these enjoyable qualities with an activity or place without realizing that the source is already available within us.

Because we don't always know that the source of our joy and freedom is already available to us, we might later say, "I miss that incredible feeling I had while hiking last week. I'll have to wait until my next vacation to return there." Yet, if we try to recreate an experience by doing the same activity again, our expectation may keep us from relaxing the seeking mind enough to allow effortless mindfulness to be revealed.

Without knowing it, most of us do our favorite leisure activities to experience effortless mindfulness and its natural qualities of freedom and joy. We do what we love to experience effortless mindfulness. However, effortless mindfulness and its qualities are not dependent on what we do or where we are. So even at work or in the New York City subway, we can discover the inner freedom, love, and clarity that are who we truly are.

GLIMPSE **Memory Door**

First, read this mindful glimpse below. Next, choose a memory of a time you felt a sense of freedom, connection, and well-being. Then do this mindful glimpse using your memory as a door to discover the effortless mindfulness that is already here now.

1. Close your eyes. Picture a time when you felt well-being while doing something active like hiking in nature. In your mind, see and feel every detail of that day. Hear the sounds, smell the smells, and feel the

air on your skin; notice the enjoyment of being with your companions or by yourself; recall the feeling of walking those last few yards toward your destination.

2. Visualize and feel yourself as you have reached your goal and are looking out over the wide-open vista. Feel that openness, connection to nature, sense of peace and well-being. Having reached your goal, feel what it's like when there's no more striving and nothing to do. See that wide-open sky with no agenda to think about, and then simply stop. Feel this deep sense of relief and peace.

3. Now, begin to let go of the visualization, the past, and all associated memories slowly and completely. Remain connected to the joy of being that is here within you.

4. As you open your eyes, feel how the well-being that was experienced then is also here now. It does not require you to go to any particular place in the past or the future once it's discovered within and all around. ■

Effortless Mindfulness Is Like a Flow State

Effortless mindfulness is not only experienced during meditation or relaxation. When we open into it, we find a new balance between being and doing. In this age of multitasking, *effortlessness* may be hard to understand, let alone value. There is a Chinese phrase, *wei wu wei*, often translated as "effortless effort" or "effortless doing," which is activity that is natural and in harmony with everything. In Tibetan Buddhism, effortless mindfulness is sometimes called *non-meditation* because we discover the spontaneous flow of wisdom and action. Effortless mindfulness is compatible with an active, engaged life since it can be practiced with eyes open, anywhere. You can look out of your window at work and, in a few minutes, shift from a sense of feeling worried or fearful into effortless well-being and compassionate connection. You can return to your activity, now operating from effortless mindfulness.

You may know a form of effortless mindfulness as "being in the zone" or in a flow state. Flow is one of the most important areas of research in contemporary psychology. Many of us consider flow an optimal way of functioning while doing complex tasks. In 1990, psychologist Mihaly Csikszentmihalyi, PhD, published his seminal book, *Flow: The Psychology of Optimal Experience*, based on years of research. Csikszentmihalyi and his team studied the ways people engage in sports, art, music, scientific research, and other tasks in order to enter a state of flow.

Csikszentmihalyi points to these seven qualities of flow:

- Knowing that an activity is doable, that our skills are adequate to the task

- Being completely involved in and focused on what we're doing

- A sense of ecstasy

- Great inner clarity: knowing what needs to be done and how well we're doing

- A sense of serenity: no worries about oneself; a feeling of going beyond the boundaries of ego

- Timelessness: being thoroughly focused on the present so that hours seem to pass in minutes

- Intrinsic motivation: whatever produces flow becomes its own reward[1]

Most people master the task they are good at to enter the flow state. But in effortless mindfulness, we first shift into an integrated flow state, and then we can do any task from heart knowing.

GLIMPSE **From Your Heart**

1. Pause . . . notice your next out-breath . . . then,
   with the next in-breath, let your awareness
   move from your head down to your heart.

2. What is it like to know from your heart? ■

Introducing Awake Awareness

To practice any form of mindfulness, we shift our awareness and level of mind to see things differently. Deliberate mindfulness uses attention and our observing mind, whereas effortless mindfulness comes from a particular level of mind and awareness that is not as familiar. Among other names, this unique level of mind and awareness has been called source of mind, nature of mind, unity consciousness, natural awareness, true nature, optimal mind, and heart-mind. I will call this level of awareness and mind *awake awareness*.

Awake awareness is the foundation of knowing, like the quantum field from which individual particles of thoughts or waves of feelings appear. Awake awareness is formless and contentless, yet knowing. At first, awake awareness feels like the absence of thought and an opening into more space. Then, we notice an alertness, a clarity, and a feeling as if we are aware from the open space. It's not the same experience as knowing from thought, and it does not feel like "I" am aware. It is more as if we've shifted into an awareness that is already awake by itself, without our help. This is why it is called *awake* awareness.

Here's a deeper look at what awake awareness is and isn't:

- Awake awareness is our primary level of knowing, which is prior to thinking, includes thinking, and is also beyond thinking.

- Awake awareness is not an altered, transcendent, or even a meditative state. It is not attention, and it's not *mindful* awareness; neither is it mindlessness or zoning out.

- There are many types of consciousness (patterns of experience) such as emotional consciousness, hearing consciousness, and thinking consciousness. Awake awareness is what makes consciousness conscious. Thoughts, feelings, and sensations are dancing patterns made of awake awareness.

- Awake awareness is clear and open, resting as peace of mind, while trusting that information or insight will come when needed.

- Awake awareness is the same in all of us, yet our individuality arises from it. Rather than looking to our thoughts, memories, personality, or roles to identify ourselves, through effortless mindfulness we come to know awake awareness as the primary dimension of who we are. Once we experience awake awareness as the foundation of our identity, we experience our conditioned thoughts, emotions, and sensations as waves within the ocean of our life.

- Awake awareness cannot be harmed by any strong emotional state. In other words, awake awareness is the source from which all emotional states arise and are experienced. We don't have to leave or change our feelings to find essential well-being.

- Awake awareness is nonconceptual, invisible, formless, boundless, and timeless, yet it is our optimal level of knowing and the foundation of our identity. It is experienced in those times when we peek beyond the veil of our conventional experience and notice the silence that is the fabric of our everyday reality.

- Awake awareness unfolds into open-hearted awareness, and then the natural qualities of well-being, compassion, and intuitive intelligence are revealed.

Awake awareness is the most important discovery we can make on our path of effortless mindfulness. However, in this approach, awake awareness is not the end goal, and we do not seek to remain in a detached witness state or a state of pure awareness. Instead, awake awareness will unfold into awake awareness-energy embodied and into open-hearted awareness. Similarly, as we will explore later in this book, effortless mindfulness could be called "effortless mindfulness embodied" or "effortless heart mindfulness" as we learn to live an awakened life.

GLIMPSE **Background Awareness**

1. Take one slow, deep breath.

2. Let out a sigh.

3. Now, let your awareness open to discover the background awareness that is already effortlessly awake and aware without your help.

4. Notice that you can effortlessly focus *from* this background awareness. ■

The practice of effortless mindfulness begins as a simple shift or letting go to discover a naturally awake awareness that is already present all around and within us. One of my students described the experience like this: "I'm not aware of an open mind and an open heart. I'm aware *from* an open mind and heart that is connected to everything." When we tap into this feeling of viewing from our wordless awake awareness, it opens us to a relief from suffering, natural joy, and compassionate connection with people and the world around us.

We have been taught that our intelligence, identity, and safety are based on developing and being centered in thought-based knowing, or what I will call our *small mind*. When we shift from our small mind to awake awareness as the source of mind, we discover that we are already effortlessly mindful. Effortless mindfulness is the way of knowing, creating, and relating from awake awareness. Although effortless mindfulness begins by letting go of everything, we ultimately become embodied, energetic, loving, and fully human.

GLIMPSE **Eyes of Awareness**

1. With a soft gaze, simply see what is here in front of you.

2. Notice the awareness that is looking through your eyes.

3. Now close your eyes and notice the same awareness that was looking out is still here.

4. Simply rest as this wordless awareness, which is now aware of itself.

5. Without creating a thinker, be the awareness that welcomes and includes everything. ■

Why We Haven't Discovered Our Greatest Natural Gift

You might be asking: If awake awareness as the source of effortless mindfulness is already here, why haven't I discovered it yet? This is a good question. One reason we don't discover it is that we don't have awake awareness on most of our Western psychological maps. Many people who have longed and strived to be free of suffering have missed awake awareness, not because they lacked desire or commitment but because they didn't know what to look for or where to look.

The Shangpa Kagyu tradition of Tibetan Buddhism gives four insightful reasons we don't naturally discover awake awareness, which I find quite helpful:

1. Awake awareness is so close that you can't see it.

2. Awake awareness is so subtle that you can't understand it.

3. Awake awareness is so simple that you can't believe it.

4. Awake awareness is so good that you can't accept it.

Let's take a closer look at each of these:

1. "So close that you can't see it" means that awake awareness is hidden in plain sight. It is closer than our own breath. We can't find awake awareness because awake awareness is not an "it." Awake awareness is neither an object nor thing that can be seen, heard, touched, smelled, or tasted. It isn't a thought, emotion, image, belief, feeling, or even energy. Awake awareness is invisibly inherent within us and is where we're looking from. We need to learn how to have awake awareness look within, turn around, or rest back, so that awake awareness can discover itself. Then, awake awareness is the source of mind from which we are able to perceive.

2. "So subtle that you can't understand it" means we can't know awake awareness with our thinking mind. Neither the five senses, the thinking mind, the ego, the will, the imagination, nor attention can *know* awake awareness. Just as the eye cannot hear sounds, thinking and attention cannot know awake awareness. Only awake awareness can know

awake awareness. Awake awareness is experiential.
It is a more direct way of knowing that is beyond
thought or prior to thought, although it can utilize
thought when needed. What you'll discover as you do
mindful glimpses is how to separate awake awareness
from our thinking mind and have awake awareness
know directly, without using conceptual knowing.

3. "So simple that you can't believe it" because once
it's discovered, awake awareness is natural and not
complex. The only thing that makes it seem difficult
is that it's unknown—until it's discovered. Many
people who are looking for spiritual fireworks are
surprised when the "aha!" holds no drama. However,
you feel free of suffering, free from worry about
worry, free from fear of fear, and free from anger
at anger. This simplicity is why, in Zen Buddhism,
awake awareness is often called "ordinary mind."

4. "So good that you can't accept it" because you didn't
need to earn it, develop it, or be good enough to get it.
It's hard to believe that the well-being, innocence, and
basic goodness that you've been looking for is who you
truly are. Awake awareness is deeper than any shame-
based feelings or long-held beliefs of being worthless,
wrong, bad, stupid, or unlovable. You can begin to
feel an inherent sense of safety and support that you
had previously been looking for in things, people, and
achievements. It relieves you of the pressure to try to
do things perfectly or become somebody someday
so that in the amorphous future you will be okay.
Discovering awake awareness as the source of mind and
the foundation of our identity is such a precious feeling
that some people have tears of joy upon finally feeling
it: you get to come home to who you have always been.

GLIMPSE **The Peace Within**

What is here now if the peace you are seeking is already here? ■

Awakening as the Next Natural Stage of Human Development

The way of effortless mindfulness is one approach to living from awareness and compassion. Effortless mindfulness begins as a meditation practice but becomes a holistic way of sustaining our most optimal way of living—the shift that has traditionally been called *awakening*. It's a term shared by many religions, used by spiritual teachers, and studied by historians. In the introduction, I defined awakening as "a shift and upgrade of awareness, mind, and self." A fuller definition of awakening is moving from our current, limited mind and small self to a new, upgraded operating system of optimal mind and expansive, interconnected Self.

The term *awakening* is an apt one because people who've had the experience report that it resembles waking from a dream. We spend much of our lives sleepwalking while hoping the project of improving and developing our separate sense of self will help us feel happy and connected. When we wake up from this daydream, we may be surprised to realize that our limited perspective is only a small part of a vaster reality.

Awakening may seem like a distant, unattainable goal or a lofty challenge, but it's no more unreachable than any other stage of learning and growth that you've already lived through. Awakening is not limited to those who join a monastery, live in a cave, or are Olympic athletes of meditation. After working with thousands of meditation students and psychotherapy clients as well as colleagues who teach meditation, neuroscience, and developmental psychology, what I've learned is this: awakening is the next, natural stage of human development.

There are many ways to awaken. Some are spontaneous and may occur during a time of great peace and connection with a beloved or with nature. Some occur during a time of heartbreak and hopelessness, and more than one person has told me that as they were having a breakdown they had a *breakthrough*. However it happens, the small mind and small self reach their limits, and awake awareness shines through. Effortless mindfulness is a practice that leads to and supports awakening.

Initially, we *wake up* from the small mind and small sense of self and into awake awareness as the boundless ground—the unity of the infinite and the finite. Then, we *wake into* an embodied, interconnected feeling of flow and being home. Then, we *wake out* to natural, creative, and compassionate activity and relationship with others.

I believe that awakening is a natural stage of human development and that we need to humbly and honestly share stories with each other about our own growth in this regard so that we can open the conversation and normalize this concept in our culture. For me, initial awakening was a radical shift to uncover an essential dimension of well-being, a feeling that everything is ultimately okay, that who I essentially am is okay. This realization is nothing like imagination, belief, or a temporary meditation state. Although awake awareness is invisible, the knowing that "all is well" is as real and intimate as the feeling of my body breathing. What is revealed with awakening is a sense of interconnection with everyone and a realization that we are essentially the same. It feels like unconditional love, as if there are no circumstances that could change this emotion. The new view is from a tenderhearted presence that is here, even when challenging things are happening. Over the years, with consistent practice of effortless mindfulness, this foundation of freedom, well-being, and unconditional love has become the new normal for me and many of my colleagues and students. With practice, it can become yours as well.

The way of effortless mindfulness is practiced through small glimpses of awake awareness as a way to fine-tune our consciousness in the midst of our day. When we get caught in thought, we can "learn to return" and "train to remain" as our awakened nature. After a series of small glimpses, many times, effortless mindfulness becomes "second nature." We trust the feeling of knowing and talking from what feels like a continuous intuition. We "know by heart" without the paralysis of analysis, like gliding down a hill on a bicycle with our hands off the handlebar.

GLIMPSE **How to Do Not-Doing**

Can you let go into the awake awareness that is resting deeper than sleep, yet wide awake? ∎

On Our Way to Effortless Mindfulness

As in any learning process, there are obstacles, traps, or points of difficulty that everyone encounters. One of them is our doubt, thinking something like, "Other people are getting it, but I'm not." However, the interesting thing about effortless mindfulness is that your doubting part, your sincere effort–making part, and your thinking mind will never get it. If you think, "I will never get this," in some ways you are correct because the "I" that is trying to "get it" can't.

If you had never ridden a bicycle, I could describe how to ride: put your left leg on the left pedal, then swing your right leg over the bike, push off, and begin to move before you put your foot on the right pedal, and then pedal as you try to balance and keep your hands steady on the handle grips. It can make some sense, but it's only when you get on the bicycle, start riding, and get a feel for it yourself that you will know balance and effortless riding.

Ultimately, you don't need to intellectually understand how to do effortless mindfulness any more than you need to understand the physics behind how your body balances when you ride a bicycle. You need only to shift into awake awareness as the place of knowing. From there, the knowing will teach itself.

Try the following mindful glimpse to experience these teachings more fully.

GLIMPSE **Relax the Problem Solver**

To begin this glimpse, start from wherever you are. Notice the sense of "me" that is here now. Notice the feeling of having a sense of self as a doer or problem solver. The small sense of self keeps its centrality by being a problem solver. It can be helpful in solving everyday problems, but it is mainly trying to solve the problem of identity, which it can't do. This manager part is usually felt within your body looking out of your eyes. Notice the location, shape, size, and feeling of this "me" that is trying to be helpful and undertake this mindful glimpse. It usually has thoughts and worries like, "Am I doing it right?" or "I don't think I will get it," or "How do I do this?"

The goal is not to escape everyday problems, situations, or issues that need to be dealt with. Instead, experience what it's like to step out of the problem-solver identity: relax this manager and notice what's here. When awareness looks directly, notice what changes. What is absent and what new qualities arise? What is the new feeling of what or who is here?

1. With open or closed eyes, ask yourself: *What is here now when there is no problem to solve?*

2. Let your awareness unhook from the problem solver, drop, open, feel within and all around. Who is here? What is aware? What is here when there is nowhere to go and nothing to do? Nothing to know or create or become? What is here, just now, when you are not the problem solver? What is here when you are not orienting by thought, you are not going down to sleep, and you are not going back to daydream? Just feel; what is this?

3. Now, ask yourself: *What's aware now, when there is no problem to solve?*

4. Feel the qualities that arise. What's absent that was here a few minutes ago? What natural qualities are here now?

5. Where are you aware from? What is this feeling of being?

6. Now, from fresh beginner's mind, inquire: *What's here now when there's no problem to solve?* ■

In the next chapter, we will look more closely at what is unique about effortless mindfulness by comparing it with the more well-known form of deliberate mindfulness.

2

Discovering Effortless Mindfulness

In general, mindfulness can be defined as a way of being conscious of our internal and external experiences, of being engaged and related to what we are doing. The opposite of mindfulness is mindlessness: being distracted, spaced-out, or impulsive. It's doing things without thinking about them, not being clear about our words or actions. Mindfulness is a basic human capacity and has become part of contemporary Western culture as we have joined millions of people around the world who have been practicing mindfulness for millennia.

Mindfulness is one of the most important things we can discover for our health and happiness, and over the past twenty years, empirical research has repeatedly shown that it reduces stress-related symptoms, anxiety, depression, and chronic pain as well as improving cognitive function, boosting immunity, and lowering blood pressure. Mindfulness is now taught in schools, community centers, hospitals, gyms, prisons, and businesses. Gradually, mindfulness meditation as a basic tool of healthy living is becoming as routine as eating well, exercising, and getting enough sleep.

When I look back at my life, I realize my mindfulness training began when I was quite young, while playing sports and doing art projects in elementary school. My first formal meditation instruction was in Transcendental Meditation (TM) when I was sixteen. During college, I practiced Christian contemplation, attended Quaker meetings, and went on a Zen retreat. When I attended graduate school for a master's degree in psychology and spirituality, I traveled to Sri Lanka, India, and Nepal on a fellowship to study varieties of meditation and healing. It was during that year, over three decades ago, that I was fortunate enough to be introduced to both deliberate and effortless mindfulness. I started by spending six months at the University of Peradeniya near Kandy, Sri Lanka, and in monasteries and meditation centers practicing *vipassana*, or insight meditation, from the Theravada Buddhist tradition, all forms of meditation that I call "deliberate mindfulness."

Later, I traveled to India, where I heard the Dalai Lama give a public talk about direct path—or essence—traditions in Tibetan Buddhism, called Dzogchen and Mahamudra. He taught that the love and freedom we all seek is already equally within all of us, and there are ways to directly realize awake awareness as their source. I was so moved by his teaching that I enthusiastically raised my hand and asked who I could study this direct path with. He suggested a teacher, Tulku Urgyen Rinpoche in Nepal. I changed my plans and traveled by train, bus, and plane to meet with him at his hermitage on the slopes of the Kathmandu Valley.

It was through this teacher that I first heard the term *effortless mindfulness*. In his book *Rainbow Painting*, Tulku Urgyen Rinpoche writes that "there are two types of mindfulness: deliberate and effortless."[1] He described effortless mindfulness as a simple yet advanced form of mindfulness. He taught that effortless mindfulness is the path to realizing and living from our nature of mind (awake awareness).

In Tibetan Buddhism, *rigpa* is the word for "nature of mind," or awake awareness. Its opposite is *marigpa*, or "not rigpa," which is the root of suffering. The cause of suffering is failure to recognize awake awareness, and the solution to suffering is in realizing and living from awake awareness. The shift into awake awareness is what makes effortless mindfulness possible.

When I met with Tulku Urgyen Rinpoche, he was sixty-one years old and had completed three separate three-year retreats in his lifetime. However, he explained that his uncle and teacher had shown him how to directly access effortless mindfulness when he was eleven years old, and he said that what he had experienced through the practice when he was young and what he experienced through those years-long retreats seem to be exactly the same.[2] He shared that this was one of the reasons he offered direct practices of effortless mindfulness to those who might be interested and ready to access their natural source of mind immediately.

When Tulku Urgyen Rinpoche first gave a small group of us effortless mindfulness instructions, it took only a few minutes. Yet I became as calm and clear as after my ten-day deliberate mindfulness meditation retreats in Sri Lanka. But it was also a different type of calm. I felt alert, compassionate, embodied, and energetically connected to everyone and everything. My emotions were more accessible and spacious, and I related to them directly in a loving way. I began to laugh as tears of gratitude flowed down my face. The pervasive feeling of anxiety, self-centeredness, and fear, which had always felt like a normal part of who I was, dissolved. What was here instead was a profound sense of well-being, unity, joy, and gratitude. This full expression lasted through the day and had faded a bit when I awoke the next morning, but it remained in the background, and, more importantly, something fundamental had changed in me.

Deliberate and Effortless Mindfulness

Because effortless mindfulness is a less familiar approach for most Westerners, it may be easier to understand it in contrast with the more familiar deliberate mindfulness, which is now so widespread that it is what most people call "mindfulness." Most of the mindfulness books, centers, and teachers in the West have come from the Theravada and some Zen traditions.

In my own journey from the Theravada tradition in Sri Lanka to the Tibetan tradition in Nepal, I could see these were different approaches to meditation. It's important to say that both of these traditions have the same goal of awakening; they are simply different paths up the same mountain. I started with good training in deliberate mindfulness, and I am glad I had this period of deliberate mindfulness practice because I benefited from the wonderful teachers I studied with. Because of this experience with both traditions, I am able to help most people start their meditation practice with either deliberate or effortless mindfulness. I refer those who do not resonate with the effortless mindfulness approach to insight meditation or Zen meditation centers to learn forms of deliberate mindfulness. Just as my friends and colleagues have generously translated and brought deliberate mindfulness to our culture, I would like to offer a contemporary approach to effortless mindfulness to help people relieve suffering.

The word *effortless* isn't simply modifying what is usually understood as mindfulness—like *easy* listening or *instant* coffee. We aren't being asked to try to be effortless. (Trying to be effortless can be quite an effort!) Effortless mindfulness does not mean that there is not an initial effort. We learn how to make an initial effort to shift out of our small mind to find an effortless awareness that is already here. It is also called "effortless" because mindfulness becomes spontaneously sustaining.

Effortless mindfulness involves as much unlearning as learning to uncover our natural well-being. The goal of effortless mindfulness is not to escape or transcend but to live a fully intimate human life. The immediate goal of effortless mindfulness is to transition into the new, upgraded operating system, which is embodied and open-hearted and has greater capacity to be with our full human experience. One student of mine reported, "I am feeling a deep sense that all is well, that who I am is okay. It's not that there are not difficulties and pain, but now I feel a loving support within that gives me new motivation."

In deliberate mindfulness, we intentionally cultivate a loving attitude, calm our small thinking mind, and then observe our thoughts and feelings. In effortless mindfulness, we shift out of our small thinking mind into the source of mind, which is already calm, focused, interconnected, and compassionate. The radical discovery is that the freedom, clarity, and natural love we seek are always right here. This natural awareness does not have to be created but simply uncovered. We don't have to believe our shame-based stories and culture that we are unworthy and unlovable. Instead, the report from those who have looked within using effortless mindfulness is that basic goodness is the foundation of who we are. On the level of our essential nature, there is nowhere to go and nothing to develop. The practice of effortless mindfulness is learning how to discover, uncover, realize, or awaken to this hidden foundation of who we are.

In the Mahamudra tradition, the practices of deliberate mindfulness are usually taught in the beginning. However, effortless mindfulness can also be taught first, for those who are drawn to it. I have found it takes about the same amount of time to learn as deliberate mindfulness, and when you begin with effortless mindfulness, you still get all the benefits of deliberate mindfulness.

To look more closely at the difference between these two kinds of mindfulness, consider a widely accepted definition of deliberate mindfulness from Jon Kabat-Zinn, one of the important teachers to help bring mindfulness into contemporary culture:

Mindfulness means paying attention in a particular way: on purpose, in the present moment, and nonjudgmentally.[3]

Here is my definition of effortless mindfulness:

Effortless mindfulness is letting go of thoughts, present moments, and attention—opening to a naturally compassionate, nonconceptual awake awareness that is interconnected here and Now.

When we compare these two types of mindfulness, we see that there are several significant distinctions between deliberate mindfulness and effortless mindfulness:

- In effortless mindfulness, rather than "paying" attention, we are *letting go* of attention to receive another kind of awareness, namely awake awareness.

- In effortless mindfulness, rather than paying attention "on purpose," we are relaxing the goal-oriented mindful meditator to discover a nonconceptual awake awareness that is aware and focused without our help.

- In effortless mindfulness, rather than starting by concentrating or narrowing focus "in a particular way" on an object like our breath, we are *opening to* awareness as the object and the subject, to discover a spacious, contentless awareness from which we are mindful. Rather than taming the horses of our mind in a small enclosure, we are opening the gate to the field of spacious awake awareness.

- When we shift into effortless mindfulness, rather than trying to create a "nonjudgmental" attitude, we discover that awake awareness is not just neutrally nonjudgmental but is a *naturally compassionate* dimension of who we are.

- Rather than "paying attention" to an object from a detached mindful witness, effortless mindfulness feels intimately and energetically *interconnected* with what we're aware of. Effortless mindfulness is aware of our body, emotions, and thoughts from within and all around.

- Deliberate mindfulness practice actively cultivates the attitude of lovingkindness, whereas in effortless mindfulness, we discover a *natural lovingkindness* that is already here. This discovery of natural lovingkindness is the foundation of a new motivation for compassionate activity that is not based on external rules but comes from the direct experience of interconnection with all of life.

From the perspective of effortless mindfulness, you can't be in the present moment. Rather than paying attention "in the present moment," effortless mindfulness is being aware of present moments coming and going *here and Now*. This is a big difference, not trying to be in the moment or even just watching the changing moments that arise and pass. The Now is not the present moment. The Now is not the present time, either. The Now is timeless time that is aware of past, present, and future. The Now does not come and go and treats past, present, and future as similar relative experiences. So, in the Now, we can be aware of the coming and going of present moments while we make plans for the future or recall the past.

Remembering Who We Are

The origin of the word *mindfulness* comes from a word in the Pali language, *sati*, which is translated literally as "remembering." In deliberate mindfulness, it means remembering to return our attention to the object of meditation, like breath, when attention wanders. Attention is defined by Merriam-Webster as "the act or state of applying the mind to something."[4] You can apply your small mind to your breath or a task, but eventually the small mind will wander, and you will become distracted. Maintaining continuous attention is difficult, not just because the attention does not remain stable but because the small mind is not a stable entity. American psychologist William James agreed: "There is no such thing as voluntary attention sustained for more than a few seconds at a time. What is called sustained voluntary attention is a repetition of successive efforts which bring back the topic to the mind."[5]

Deliberate mindfulness is being attentive from our small mind or a mindful witness; it requires us to continuously return to the task—re-remembering and refocusing. The reason we lose focus when we try to be mindful is not lack of willpower. We lose focus because the small mind we're looking from is always moving and changing. In deliberate mindfulness, we must continuously reapply ourselves to the task at hand by actively remembering not only to focus but to recreate a "focuser" identity in our mind.

In effortless mindfulness, sati (mindfulness) is a different kind of remembering. Effortless mindfulness is a remembering of our true nature—who we have always been. In effortless mindfulness, we don't have to pay attention from our small mind because we are aware from awake awareness, or source of mind, which is not made of moving thoughts. We can feel in a flow with a wider context but also a feeling of being grounded and not overwhelmed by the things that are happening. A client told me, "I feel grounded, but it's interesting because the supportive ground is made of awareness. From here, I feel interconnected and effortlessly focused. And that gives me a sense of deep safety and well-being."

Rather than cleaning up and calming the stormy clouds of our mind first, effortless mindfulness starts with recognizing awake awareness, which is already naturally calm and clear. Then we can return to our stormy problems or challenges with a new perspective and sense of well-being. The benefit of this is that awake awareness is the only thing that can truly bear that which seemed unbearable. When we are mindful from our awake awareness, we have effortless focus, which is not distracted by thoughts, feelings, or sensations. This is often what students first report upon learning effortless mindfulness: "I feel open and connected without anything able to distract my focus." The conceptual small mind doesn't become wiser, nor can the calm, focused small mind know awake awareness. With effortless mindfulness, we learn to shift out of small mind into awake awareness, which already has a calm, compassionate clarity.

GLIMPSE **Awake Awareness Knows Without Using Thought or Attention**

In this glimpse, instead of focusing on what we are aware of, we will have awareness be aware of itself. This may be something that has never crossed your mind. In learning about using awareness instead of attention, we will look back to the source of mind, awake awareness, and then focus from here. Instead of following the flashlight of attention out to the movie screen of experience, we see if we can feel awareness directly. We have learned to experience life as a subject looking at objects, even internal objects like thoughts and emotions. One helpful practice of deliberate mindfulness is called "mental noting." In mental noting practice, our mindful witness becomes more precise by labeling thoughts, feelings, and sensations as they arise. In this mindful glimpse, we will let go of labeling and instead learn to trust the intelligence of awake awareness. Now we will have awareness feel what awareness is like when it is both the subject and the object. It will be helpful to have this invisible, contentless awareness know itself as we separate the awareness-based knowing from thought-based knowing.

1. To begin, simply close your eyes while allowing your awareness to remain open. Feel your breath moving within your body. Feel your whole body from within while noticing your breathing happening by itself for three breaths. Be easy and comfortable. Relax while remaining alert.

2. Take a moment to see what is here now. Notice how your body is feeling. Is it uncomfortable, comfortable, agitated, relaxed, tired, or neutral? Just be aware of your body without trying to change it. Just be aware of it as it is.

3. Now simply notice what is aware of these feelings and sensations. Feel the awareness in which these sensations are happening. Rather than being aware of sensations, feel the awareness that is aware. Notice that the awareness is not tired, is not in pain, is not agitated or anxious. Feel how this awareness is with your body.

4. Now notice the activity of your mind and thoughts. Just be aware of whether your thoughts are agitated, calm, tired, emotional, anxious, or neutral. Without changing anything at all, allow your mind and thoughts to be as they are.

5. Now notice the space in which thoughts are moving. Be interested in the awareness instead of the thoughts. Shift to notice not just the content but the context. Feel the awareness that is aware. Notice how awareness allows your mind to be as it is without changing anything.

6. Begin to notice that awake awareness is alert, clear, and nonjudgmental. Feel the awareness that is not tired, anxious, or in pain. Notice that awake awareness is all around and inherent within your body and within your mind. Instead of being identified with the states of your body or mind or trying to accept or change them, simply become interested in *what* is aware.

7. What is awareness like that is already accepting of things as they are—right here and now? Notice the awareness of the next sound you hear. Does awareness have a location or size? What is it like to be aware of experiences from this pain-free, spacious awareness?

8. Now simply rest as the awareness that is aware of your thoughts and sensations. Hang out as awareness without going up to thought to know or down to sleep to rest. Be the awareness that welcomes your sensations and thoughts. Ask yourself: *Am I aware of this spacious awareness?* Or *What's it like when I'm aware from this spacious awareness, which is welcoming thoughts, feelings, and sensations?* Notice that the awareness is aware from all around and from within—spacious and pervasive.

9. Just let go of focusing on any one thing. Be aware of everything without labeling. Feel that your awareness is no longer knowing from thought. Feel what it is like to be aware from awareness, which includes your thoughts and sensations from head to toe.

10. Simply let be and remain uncontracted and undistracted, welcoming without effort. ■

Two Levels of Mind

One simple way to distinguish the two types of mindfulness is to say that they are both being mindful but from different levels of mind. This is important because what you can be mindful of depends on what level of mind you're mindful from. In effortless mindfulness, it is not as important to focus on what thoughts and emotions are arising but rather to ask, "Who or what level of mind are they arising to?" In effortless mindfulness, we shift from focusing on what we are aware of into focusing on awareness itself—moving from a detached observer and into a view from interconnected awake awareness.

In deliberate mindfulness, we are aware, from our mindful witness, of things arising and passing. Effortless mindfulness invites us to be more intimately interconnected with our experience and all that is happening. This begins when we shift out of both our conceptual mind and our mindful witness and into awake awareness. Deliberate mindfulness focuses on the *contents* of consciousness, while effortless mindfulness turns back to be aware of the *context*—awareness itself. With deliberate mindfulness, we discover who we are not. With effortless mindfulness, we discover who we essentially are.

Effortless mindfulness does not lead to being detached from emotions but rather to both feeling more vulnerable and to having more capacity to be tender and welcoming of all feelings. The radical reports from my students are that our essential nature is loving, joyous, and free of worry, and we just need to untie the knots of conditioning to reveal these natural qualities.

One student who came to a daylong retreat was a dance and yoga teacher, originally trained in Russia as a ballerina. She said she had never before done a practice like effortless mindfulness. Near the end of the day, after doing a variety of effortless mindfulness glimpses, she said, "I am crying with joy because, for the first time in my life, I am able to intentionally feel fully embodied. This feeling of being aware of my body from within and from everywhere only happens once in a while. Embodiment is not just being in my body, but feeling connected to everything and everybody. It is what I love most about yoga and dance, and I chase it, but I never knew how to access it directly until now."

Leaving the Witness Protection Program

In deliberate mindfulness, after an initial stage of calming our chattering mind, we establish a mindful witness to observe thoughts, feelings, and sensations. Insight meditation can lead to an important insight that "I am not my thoughts, beliefs, stories, or a thought-based identity." This is what I call the *mindful move*. The mindful move helps us get a healthy distance from being identified with emotions and thoughts. For example, we may feel misunderstood by a family member and respond with defensive anger only to realize that we misunderstood what they said. The mindful move can allow just enough space to ask a question that can bring clarity to you and the relationship. We see that there is not a solid mind and not a solid separate self, made of thoughts, by observing thoughts like, "I am thinking this thought." This helps us take thoughts less personally.

Many people seek mindfulness training because of suffering caused by being too attached. Some people who come to my workshops for the first time say they are too identified with their thoughts and feelings: "I wake up every morning immediately worried about work, then get involved in dramas, which causes more stress." Or, "I feel like I'm hypersensitive to other people's moods and take on their feelings." We make the mindful move to a detached witness with deliberate mindfulness. Establishing this mindful witness brings relief from being overidentified, which is an important step. However, the danger of stopping at this level of a detached witness is that we may end up isolated, as if in a "witness protection program." One student said, "I was good at being mindful of activities from my birds-eye-view, but I began to feel I lost my flow and became more aloof, mental, and robotic, like Spock from *Star Trek*."

Here, there's still a subtle dualism of "observer" and "observed" that gives us a feeling of freedom from attachment while maintaining a feeling of looking down from a distant tower at our body, mind, and the world. The unique thing about effortless mindfulness is that the first shift is to look back through the meditator to even further disidentification as we open to vast, timeless, nonconceptual awake awareness. The unfolding of effortless mindfulness continues to become aware simultaneously from outside and within, so we feel a natural interconnection and intimacy with everything without being reidentified.

The Effortless Mindfulness Research

Deliberate mindfulness has two main styles of practice: *shamatha*, translated as "calm abiding," and *vipassana*, translated as "insight meditation." First, there is calming and focusing of the small mind in calm abiding. Next are insight meditation practices, like the Four Foundations of Mindfulness (which I'll explain in the next chapter), where we establish a mindful monitor to witness the contents of consciousness.

It is now accepted in the field of mindfulness research to refer to calm abiding as *focused attention* (FA) and the insight meditation practice as *open monitoring* (OM). Recently, a third type of mindfulness, *nondual awareness* (NDA), has been included in mindfulness research studies.

The term *nondual* is one of the best ways to describe effortless mindfulness. The Sanskrit word for *nonduality* is *advaita*, which means "not two." It is pointing to the view that the dualistic way of perceiving—inside versus outside, subject versus object, and other versus self—is not the only level of reality. In Buddhism, *nondual* is defined as "two truths," meaning that ultimate reality as formless awake awareness and everyday relative reality are experienced simultaneously. Some people define *nonduality* as "oneness" or "pure awake awareness" because it is beyond dualistic thought. Here, nonduality means that the dualistic relative reality we experience, of separate energies and things, is made of awake awareness. So awake awareness and appearances are not essentially two different things.

Nonduality begins with a recognition of a transcendent dimension of reality—awake awareness—and then sees this as the foundation of our everyday dimension of reality. So when we shift into nondual awareness, we experience objects both as interconnected and as a unique expression simultaneously. Nondual awareness is another way of describing the view from effortless mindfulness. Here are three descriptions that might be helpful to understand the difference in these three stages of mindfulness. Focused attention (FA) is like looking down from a tower to the river of your breath. Open monitoring (OM) is like looking from an open sky to thoughts, feelings, and sensations as separate objects, like clouds and birds, coming and going. Nondual awareness (NDA) is like being the entire ocean of awareness that is also arising as the unique wave of your body while feeling an interconnected flow with everything. For this reason, I often call effortless mindfulness *nondual mindfulness.*

In one research study, conducted in 2012 at New York University by Zoran Josipovic, PhD, and his research team, experienced practitioners of effortless mindfulness were asked to shift into nondual awareness while receiving a functional magnetic resonance imaging (fMRI) scan.[6] I am familiar with these important results because I was one of the subjects in this study. We were asked to do focused attention practices, open monitoring practices, and then nondual awareness practices. The results showed dramatic differences in the brain between the different practices, as I will explain below. The NDA practices I did while in the fMRI machine were the effortless mindfulness practices that I present in this book.

The study looked at our brain's two primary networks: the externally focused task-positive mode and the internally focused default mode. During goal-oriented activity, the default mode network is deactivated, and the task-positive network is activated. When we are daydreaming, creatively imagining, or thinking about a situation, our internal network is activated, and our external network is deactivated. Our brain continuously and rhythmically alternates between these two networks, which leads to a feeling of distraction. We can notice this when, for instance, we are standing in line and realize our attention goes outward to what's going on in the room and then shifts to become aware of something we're thinking about. We are not intentionally doing this; our brain is alternating, and our attention follows.

One insight from Josipovic's study was that one-pointed focused attention (FA) tends toward "suppression of the activity of the default network."[7] FA and OM each suppress one of the two brain modes. While suppressing one mode gives us relief, we cannot function for long from just one mode. If we are only focused on monitoring our inner world (OM), we cannot complete daily tasks; if we are only mindful of outer tasks (FA), we can become unaware of our inner life and lose the creativity that comes from free association and creative thinking. Josipovic writes that "NDA meditation is different from FA and OM meditations in that it enables an atypical state of mind in which extrinsic and intrinsic experiences are increasingly synergistic rather than competing." Effortless mindfulness balances the activity of the default-mode network and task-positive network so that we are equally aware of what we're doing and our internal state. Awake awareness is aware of what happens both inside and outside.

We don't want to completely shut down the default-mode network because it has positive aspects, including giving us the ability to imagine, free-associate, and think creatively. These advanced creative abilities distinguish us from other creatures as they enable us to imagine future outcomes and plan for them—an evolutionary advantage that we would lose if we were to repress the default-mode network entirely to make ourselves calm.

The study concluded that FA practices, such as one-pointed meditation, create calm by keeping the one mode of the task-positive network on and suppressing the internal, default-mode network. NDA, in contrast, was shown to balance external and internal networks. For me as a subject, NDA (or effortless mindfulness) is the experience of being undistracted without effort, aware of what's going on inside and outside as a continuous, interconnected, seamless flow.

Awakening Is Restful and Creative

Another important study, done in 2018 by Poppy L. A. Schoenberg, Andrea Ruf, John Churchill, Daniel Brown, and Judson Brewer, looked at the EEG signals of practitioners who were doing similar effortless mindfulness practices.[8]

The EEG distinguishes five main types of waves, each with its own frequency. The slowest wave is delta, which oscillates between one and four cycles per second and occurs primarily during deep sleep. The next slowest, theta, occurs during a drowsy state before sleep. Alpha waves indicate relaxation and occur when there is little thinking. Beta waves are the next fastest and accompany thinking or concentration. Gamma waves are the fastest brain wave and occur during moments in which separate brain regions are firing in harmony, such as moments of insight, creativity, or "aha!" experiences.

The most significant outcome was that the frequency was in the high gamma range in all twenty-nine subjects doing forms of effortless mindfulness. The study is also striking because "in contrast to using number of hours or years of practice . . . the primary eligibility requirement was that each subject had the ability to shift from everyday mind to awake awareness."[9] This is important in showing that awakening training is possible in the midst of daily life rather than only for full-time yogis or those in monasteries.

Whether we start with deliberate or effortless mindfulness, there is a way to become effortlessly mindful in our daily lives such that we feel connected, creative, and compassionate. In the next chapter, I'll teach the effortless mindfulness versions of well-known deliberate mindfulness practices.

3

Awakening Glimpse by Glimpse

My introduction to the immediate effects of effortless mindfulness in Nepal allowed me to see that I did not need to remain in the East, join a monastery, or practice in a cave to discover the well-being, clarity, and open-hearted awareness that were already within me. I returned to the United States to continue to train with eyes open in the midst of my day-to-day life.

I have no doubt, as I look back now, that it was the natural compassion of open-hearted awareness revealed by effortless mindfulness that propelled me to pursue a second master's degree in clinical social work. As I felt a deeper connection to everyone, I wanted to train for a life of service to those most in need. I also got sober, went to weekly psychotherapy, continued psychotherapist training, and got married to the love of my life, Paige. At this time, I was also asked to join the Teachers Council of the New York Insight Meditation Center, where I taught deliberate mindfulness practices. I continued to attend teachings and retreats to develop and deepen my practices and studies with a variety of nondual and effortless mindfulness teachers.

Right after graduate school, I went to work in New York City at the Brooklyn Mental Health Clinic. This was an outpatient community center that provided psychotherapy for people who had been psychiatrically hospitalized or were living in a halfway house and attending a psychiatric day-treatment program. It was during breaks or when clients missed sessions that I began exploring and developing the mindful glimpses in this book that are versions of the ancient wisdom practices I learned during my travels.

As I gazed out the window into the open sky from my seventeenth-floor office, I began to explore my own mind to see how suffering was created and relieved. I noticed how identification with a thought, feeling, and parts of my personality collapsed my thinking into a narrow perception of both myself and others. I practiced shifting my awareness from a contracted small self to a new way of seeing and being, which was more open-minded and open-hearted. I also noticed how, when I intentionally separated awareness from thinking, I could awaken to an already spacious and interconnected view that was free of a deep kind of suffering.

For example, if I was feeling upset, I would acknowledge my feelings and shift awareness out of the cloud of stormy emotions and then, from this open mind and open heart, return to the emotions with a new view. This brought such relief and joy! It was like emerging from a dark tunnel to a beautiful view, except I was not only seeing the view. It was as if I were viewing from an open, quiet, loving intelligence that was connected to everything. How could this freedom be so close and yet so hidden from most people's day-to-day experience? How was it that despite all the progress humanity has made in other areas—like medicine, communication, and technology—that shifting into awake awareness was not something that was recognized and taught to everyone?

I approached these explorations of the anatomy of awareness with curiosity and wonder. It was exciting to experiment and reverse-engineer practices from the wisdom traditions I had studied in India, Sri Lanka, and Nepal. One of the approaches to awakening that I draw from, Sutra Mahamudra, originated in North India. It is a tradition that is like a bridge between the three main traditions of Buddhism: Theravada, Mahayana, and Vajrayana (Tibetan). One reason I was drawn to it is that it focuses on practices for everyday people, not just monastics, to awaken in the midst of their daily life. One of my teachers, Dzogchen Ponlop Rinpoche, wrote that Sutra Mahamudra "is seen as a profound method because it does not require any of the sophisticated and complex tantric rituals, deity yoga visualization practices, or *samayas* [vows]. Sutra Mahamudra has a tradition of skillful means that contains profound methods of directly pointing out the selfless and luminous nature of mind."[1] I began to try to translate ancient practices I had learned from many teachers and texts into accessible, contemporary language and forms. I checked in with teachers such as Traleg Rinpoche to make sure the practices were staying true to the essence of the teachings as I translated them. I also began to notice that if I remained receptive, it was as if awake awareness started showing me the anatomy and principles of awakening. I started calling these contemporary versions of ancient wisdom practices "Brooklyn Mahamudra."

Stepping Out of the Cloud of Your Mind

One way of describing the experience of glimpsing in effortless mindfulness practice is to use the metaphor of a cloud. You may have felt as if you have been living in a cloud; maybe it feels like a storm cloud a lot of the time. See if you can feel the boundary and fogginess of this cloud that you call "me." You may have been trying to feel better by cleaning up the cloud of your mind by replacing negative thoughts with positive thoughts and developing good attitudes. You may have tried to calm your body and mind to make your brain as clear as possible. Within your cloud are storms, old traumas, emotional challenges, and relationships of all types. Each time you change these things and clean up one area of the cloud, it seems that another foggy issue or thunderous problem arises.

Effortless mindfulness does not begin with dissolving the cloud, calming it, or trying to transform its contents. The glimpsing method of effortless mindfulness begins with awake awareness stepping out of the cloud, shifting, dropping, or opening to discover that you are also the open sky of awake awareness! When you shift out of this cloud of the emotional or small mind and discover this spaciousness of still, quiet, alert awareness, it's a great relief. You can realize that you are the sky, and the cloudy emotions and thoughts are everchanging weather.

Awake awareness is not just contentless space but is the actual source of intelligence and identity. Here, we experience ourselves not just as a separate, big-sky witness but also as the awake awareness arising as thoughts, feelings, sensations, and parts of us. As we reach the fullness of effortless mindfulness, we will discover open-hearted awareness and ways to naturally embrace and welcome all emotions and parts of ourselves. It is from this way of being that our stormy parts—our dark moods, angry rumblings, or fearful shadows—can truly begin to heal as they are loved back to health within this dimension of open-hearted awareness. After all, all weather comes and goes, and no storm ever hurt the sky.

Local Awareness

What is unique about the effortless mindfulness approach is the use of local awake awareness as the primary way of glimpsing and shifting levels of mind. By *local*, I mean awake awareness that is appearing in one specific area, such as your head, or connected from spacious awake awareness-energy to any object. Local awake awareness, or simply *local awareness*, is able to know awake awareness because it is never separate from it. Local awake awareness provides a tool to navigate through your own consciousness. When awake awareness appears as the boundless ocean of awareness, I call it *spacious awareness*. When awake awareness appears within a particular location, I call it *local awareness*. Local awareness and spacious awareness are two aspects of the same awake awareness.

In effortless mindfulness, it is important to learn how to separate local awareness from thinking. Local awareness is normally identified, attached, or hidden within the thinking mind, so we don't realize that they can be separate. Here I will use the word *unhook* to describe the ability of local awareness to tune out of or disidentify from the thinking mind.

This important shift of local awareness can be reached in a variety of ways, such as with the inquiry practice in the Advaita Vedanta tradition of looking to the awareness within by asking, "Who am I?" or the Chinese text *The Secret of the Golden Flower*'s technique of "turning the light of awareness around," or the Zen tradition's "taking the backward step." In Tibetan Buddhism, recognition of awake awareness as the foundation of who we are is expressed as "looking at your own face," emphasizing that when we recognize it, awake awareness is as intimate and familiar as our own face. It also suggests, instead of looking outward from your face, that finding awake awareness requires turning around to notice where we're looking from.

Five Foundations of Effortless Mindfulness

Before I introduce some effortless mindfulness versions of common deliberate mindfulness practices, I'll share a more detailed map of effortless mindfulness. As a frame of reference, let's first look at one of the main sets of practices of deliberate mindfulness, which is called the Four Foundations of Mindfulness. As the Buddhist scholar Andrew Olendzki has said, "Most practitioners of insight meditation are familiar with the four foundations of mindfulness, and know that the *Satipaṭṭhāna Sutta* . . . , the *Discourse on the Foundations of Mindfulness* is the cornerstone of the *vipassanā* [insight meditation] tradition."[2] The Four Foundations of Mindfulness are:

1. Mindfulness of body and sensations

2. Mindfulness of feelings of pleasure or displeasure about the sensations

3. Mindfulness of mind: whether grasping or aversion is present or not

4. Mindfulness of mental phenomena, like thoughts, images, and other mind objects

The focus of these practices is on observing the contents of consciousness—the experiences of feelings, sensations, and mental objects that we can notice as they arise and pass away. Through deliberate mindfulness we come to realize that these contents of consciousness are fleeting—they come and go—and there is no separate self to be found within.

In teaching effortless mindfulness, I have found it helpful to create a similar format of practices I call the Five Foundations of Effortless Mindfulness. These are contemporary variations on practices from a variety of wisdom traditions, particularly the Sutra Mahamudra approach from the Indo-Tibetan tradition. Moving through these five foundations of effortless mindfulness allows us to untie the knots of limited perception, knowing, and identity. We shift from focusing on the *contents* to focus on the *context* of consciousness—awareness itself. Rather than focusing on the *contents*, we begin the five foundations of effortless mindfulness by opening to what or who is aware of these contents.

We first shift to awake awareness as the foundation of a new level of mind. This allows us to become more energetically embodied and interconnected with everything as we move through the foundations. We continue to discover a new way of seeing and being from open-hearted awareness, to live a compassionate and creative life.

Here are the Five Foundations of Effortless Mindfulness:

1. Awareness of awake awareness

2. Awake awareness as aware of itself

3. Awareness from awake awareness-energy

4. Awake awareness-energy embodied

5. Open-hearted awareness

FOUNDATION ONE   AWARENESS *OF* AWAKE AWARENESS

The first foundation of effortless mindfulness can be discovered by unhooking local awake awareness from thought and the thinker. The radical premise here is that we are already the awake awareness that we seek. Awake awareness is currently attached to or identified with the contents of consciousness. Yet awake awareness is intelligent and the source of being, knowing, and even doing. So local awake awareness can detach or unhook from the small mind and small self and return home to nonlocal awake awareness–based knowing. Local awake awareness is to awake awareness as the air in a bubble is to the open air. Local awareness is interconnected with what it knows directly, so it replaces mental attention as a way to focus. Even though you might not intellectually understand the instructions or believe that "you" can do this, simply and curiously allow local awareness to unhook and know spacious awake awareness.

Another way to describe this first foundation of effortless mindfulness is *local awake awareness is aware of spacious awake awareness.*

FOUNDATION TWO   AWAKE AWARENESS *AS* AWARE OF ITSELF

The second foundation of effortless mindfulness is awake awareness becoming aware of itself—by itself, as itself. This movement requires going beyond all references to thinking, senses, doing, and all forms of energy to discover the contentless, timeless, empty, boundless source of knowing and being. This stage is the realization that awake awareness is always already awake by itself without any help or effort. It is the important shift to direct recognition of the new operating system—awake awareness—rather than stopping in the gap of not-knowing or no-self.

Awake awareness aware of itself requires a letting go, and the way of perceiving this shift is subtle because it is a nonconceptual way of knowing—a not-knowing that knows. This is the realization that awake awareness is the source of intelligence and the boundless ground of our essential identity. There is no need to stay in this pure awake awareness for lengthy periods of meditation, as the unhooking from small mind and opening to a vast source of mind usually takes from three seconds to three minutes, as you will see with the mindful glimpses in this book.

Another way to describe this second foundation of effortless mindfulness is *spacious awake awareness is aware* as *spacious awake awareness, which is already aware.*

FOUNDATION THREE   AWARENESS *FROM* AWAKE AWARENESS-ENERGY

The third foundation of effortless mindfulness is the stage of turning as awake awareness back to knowing things directly. We moved from foundation one (being aware of awake awareness) to foundation two (being aware as awake awareness) and arrive at foundation three: being aware *from* awake awareness-energy.

When we are aware from awake awareness of any movement inside or thing outside, we realize that we are interconnected with that which we are aware of. We discover the direct experience of formless awake awareness appearing as interconnected energetic aliveness. In Theravada Buddhism, this insight is called "interdependent arising"; in Tibetan Buddhism, it is called "one taste" or the "union of emptiness and appearance." I use the term *awareness-energy* for this feeling of the intelligent, interconnected, dynamic, all-pervasive field from which our awareness arises into form. This occurs when awake awareness begins to be aware of anything and everything: awake awareness is not a detached observer but is interconnected with what it is aware of.

In the first shift of deliberate mindfulness, we realize we are not our thoughts. This form of insight meditation is done by disidentifying with thought and creating a detached mindful witness that experiences thoughts as separate objects. In this stage of effortless mindfulness, the subject and object unify when awareness becomes aware as thoughts, feelings, sensations, and energy, without becoming reattached or reidentified. This is important because many people go from awareness of awareness to a "big-sky, no-self witness" that experiences thoughts, feelings, and sensations as if they are separate objects, like birds or clouds, moving through the sky of awareness. This no-self witness is going backward to a mindfulness state of what's called "choiceless awareness." In contrast, awareness-energy is the experience of knowing everything as dancing awake awareness, from within and all around. When awake awareness knows movement or appearance, it knows it *as* awareness-energy. Awake awareness is still the primary ground, but it is inseparable from the thoughts, feelings, and sensations that are made of awake awareness. There is a feeling of subtle unity and interconnection while simultaneously experiencing things as particular and separate on the physical level.

Another way to describe this third foundation of effortless mindfulness is *spacious awake awareness aware from awareness-energy.*

FOUNDATION FOUR   AWAKE AWARENESS-ENERGY EMBODIED

The fourth foundation of effortless mindfulness is awake awareness-energy embodied as Ground of Being. This is when awake awareness-energy moves and includes the dancing emptiness of the union of formless awake awareness and our human form. At first, form is discovered to be emptiness, and now emptiness is discovered to be form. The unique thing here is that embodiment does not mean just your particular body but knowing your body is connected to all bodies and all things. The Vietnamese Buddhist teacher Thich Nhat Hanh calls this realization "interbeing."[3]

To put it another way, awake awareness-energy is the ground of our being, but our being is not limited to our human body's boundary. We experience our no-self Self both as the ocean of awareness-energy and as the arising of the unique wave of our humanness. People who practice effortless mindfulness at this stage report feeling boundless with emotional boundaries and interconnected with a sense of embodied well-being. We feel united with all things in a web of living presence that I call the realization of the Ground of Being, the unity of the infinite and the finite.

Another way to describe this fourth foundation of effortless mindfulness is *awareness-energy aware from within and all around as all-pervasive and embodied.*

FOUNDATION FIVE   OPEN-HEARTED AWARENESS

The fifth foundation of effortless meditation is awareness from open-hearted awareness, or heart-mind. Effortless mindfulness in its fullness could be called "effortless heart-mindfulness" because knowing has shifted from conceptual, small mind to awake awareness–based knowing to being aware from open-hearted awareness. From here, local awareness replaces attention as the way to focus internally and externally in an interconnected way. From effortless mindfulness at this stage, we sense that we can know information as needed without referring to thought. We can remain at home in our heart-mind and have thoughts come to us from the office in our head via Wi-Fi.

From this stage, many people report that they feel the coming together of a boundless heart and a tender human heart. Many say that they feel like they are looking out of "the eyes of the Heart." This heart-mind is not the physical heart, heart chakra, or emotional heart but compassionate intelligence that is like a continuous intuition. They describe an experience of unconditional love, non-fear, non-worry, and non-shame. This feeling is important—both the vast openness and the quality of support—because our small mind or subpersonalities may try to scare us back to the small separate self or ego manager by saying, "This is new. This is strange. There's not a lot of chatter or information. I think there could be a danger!" The good news is that you'll be able to feel the safety of the Ground of Being as the foundation of open-hearted awareness. You can begin to welcome your fearful parts and to trust your intuitive, wise, loving intelligence.

Another way to describe this fifth foundation of effortless mindfulness is *an all-pervasive awareness-energy expressing as intelligent, interconnected, loving open-hearted awareness, which is able to focus using local awareness.*

Inner and Outer Doorways

When working through the Five Foundations of Effortless Mindfulness, I have found that it is important to acknowledge different learning styles and doorways. Some people find it easier to access awake awareness by going deeply inward, harkening to the adage "the kingdom of heaven is within," while others access awake awareness by opening outward, connecting to awake awareness that is greater than the small self. We can call these *inner* doorways and *outer* doorways. Whichever doorway we start with, we will end up being aware both from spaciousness and from within ourselves, simultaneously.

The mindful glimpses in the effortless mindfulness approach use both the outer and inner doorways to have local awareness shift through each of the Five Foundations of Effortless Mindfulness.

Transitioning from Deliberate to Effortless Mindfulness

I've developed a series of practices to help transition from deliberate to effortless mindfulness. These are initial techniques that introduce calm and focus as we work with effortless mindfulness to shift into an awake awareness–based view. They are a good entry point because deliberate mindfulness versions of these practices will be familiar to many mindfulness practitioners. They are:

- The Four Postures of Dynamic Stillness

- Focusing on the Breath from Within the Breath

- Beyond the Meditator

- Lovingkindness and Compassion Are Already Here

- Embodiment Scan

One of the advantages of starting meditation training with deliberate mindfulness is that it uses commonly understood terminology and instructions: "Bring your attention to your breath at your nostrils or belly." When we begin effortless mindfulness, we need to be patient at first to experientially learn something new: "Unhook local awareness from thought and have it move to know your jaw from within your jaw. Now have local awareness open to know the space around your body." Unhooking awareness has to be fast and direct so that awareness can separate from thinking; otherwise, we may be simply stretching attention. We do not need to intellectually understand how local awareness directly knows, any more than we need to know how we can balance on a bicycle. Similarly, we won't know what it feels like until we experience balance; we have to jump on the bike, push off, and get moving to balance and ride.

As we do these mindful glimpses, it is important to note that local awareness does the shifting through all five of the foundations. This means that shifting does not employ imagination or effort by the ego manager or the meditator. Instead, it is the intelligence and intentionality of local awareness that unhooks itself from thought. When we do this, we are not creating a meditation state; instead, it is like untying knots of consciousness that bind us to ignorance and suffering.

The key is to learn how to move local awareness or experience how local awareness moves itself. Here is the unique thing about moving local awareness: When I ask you to unhook local awareness from the cloud of thought and emotion, I am not talking to "you"—the ego mind, the manager, the small mind, or the small self. I am talking to "You"—the already awake being—and asking local awake awareness to separate out from thinking and know itself directly either within or outside your body, and eventually both. The good part is that you do not have to know how to do this. If you say, "I don't know how to do that," or "I don't think I can do that," in one sense, you will be right. That "you" can't do it! Awareness will be letting go of that "self" and shifting to the vaster, interconnected sense of who you truly are.

Not all doorways or mindful glimpses are suited for everyone, so if one does not work for you, please let it go and move on to the next doorway to see if it opens for you. Each person has a different learning style, so I have designed glimpses with inner and outer doorways that use visual, auditory, physical, perceptual, intuitive, mental, and emotional approaches.

The best way to proceed is with the curiosity of an open mind and open heart to see if awareness can disidentify with your thinking mind and move on its own. I recommend you take the following mindful glimpses slowly, step by step, so that you can experience each movement for yourself. Once you become familiar with them, you can do them anywhere and at any time of day.

The Four Postures of Dynamic Stillness

Deliberate mindfulness instructions often begin with physical posture, concentrating on how to place your body in order to sit physically still, with your back straight. In this effortless mindfulness variation, we will focus on stillness at the subtler levels of experience to feel a different kind of dynamic stillness that can include movement.

1. Find a way to sit comfortably. Take a few deep breaths and relax, as if you have just finished a day's work. Become aware of your body and breath as if they are in your awareness. Become aware of the space around you, the feeling of contacting what you are sitting on, the feeling of your body, and the motion of breath happening by itself.

2. Notice your whole body breathing. Notice that breath is happening by itself. And now notice that awareness is also happening by itself. Notice how awareness is spacious like the sky, already aware from outside *and* within your breathing body.

3. Begin to feel the first stillness of your body sitting. What is it like to be sitting on the earth with the feeling of gravity and stillness? Nothing to do and nowhere to go . . . just now. Rest your body in this one place with the stillness like a mountain.

4. Now be aware of the second stillness of space. Feel the movement of your breath. Notice the stillness of space in the pause between breaths. Feel the space in the room and between objects. Rest into the space within the moving atoms in your body. Feel the space and stillness in which everything arises and passes like clouds and birds in the sky-like space within and all around.

5. Become aware of the third stillness of water. Feel the deep knowing that your body is mostly water. Feel the depth of water inside and all around. Breathe in and feel that the ocean of water is deep and still within, even while there are waves of movement and flow.

6. Now feel the fourth stillness of awareness. Feel how that which is aware does not come and go, while everything else changes. Rest as this timeless awareness, which is what all the other stillness and movement are made of. Rest deeper than sleep as the awareness that is wide awake. Find that which is already resting without any effort to rest. Rest as the invisible awake awareness that is here now arising as space, stillness, energies, and forms. ■

GLIMPSE **Focusing on the Breath from Within the Breath**

1. Become aware of your breath in either your chest or belly as it rises and relaxes. Focus your attention there, at this one area. When your mind wanders, simply bring it back to the simple, one-pointed focus in your body as your breath rises and relaxes.

2. Now, as you are focusing on your breath at that area, feel the area where you are focusing from, usually somewhere in your head, behind your eyes. Notice both the place where the breath is rising and the place from which focusing is happening.

3. Without needing to know how you're doing it, feel like you can unhook local awareness from the area from which you are focusing. Feel local awareness, like an invisible bubble of knowing, begin to drop

downward and know your jaw directly from within
your jaw. Feel your jaw from the awareness within your
jaw, the subject and object located in the same place.

4. Now notice that local awareness can move on its own to
become aware of your throat directly from within your throat.
Notice that you are not stretching attention down from your
head to your throat. And notice that you don't need to go back
up to thought to know that you are aware of your throat from
within your throat. Just be aware of your throat from your
throat—the space, aliveness, and awareness in this one area.

5. Now feel local awareness move on its own, dropping
down below your neck to become aware of your
breath directly from within your chest or belly,
so you feel the rising and relaxing directly from
where it's happening. Feel what it's like when the
focusing and the focused are happening in the
same place. Notice that the breath is happening by
itself and that awareness is happening by itself.

6. Let local awareness stay with the breath as
awareness-energy opens to the spacious awareness
outside and within your whole body.

7. When you're ready, become aware of the space in the
room around you from the space in the room. Then
continue to let awareness open until it discovers the
feeling of an already awake awareness that is both
spacious and pervasive within your body, like a
seamless field of already awake awareness-energy.

8. Be aware from this limitless space of
timeless, boundless awake awareness.

9. Notice that as you remain spacious and limitless, you can be intimately aware of the arising awareness-energy in your body, in the room, and directly from your breath arising at the center of your body.

10. Notice that you're simultaneously aware from the limitless space, the energetic field, and your human body. Notice that you can be effortlessly focused on your breath from awake awareness without being distracted. Feel the calm, focus, clarity, and well-being from effortless mindfulness. ■

GLIMPSE **Beyond the Meditator**

In this effortless mindfulness version of insight meditation, we are going to go beyond the view from the meditator. We'll begin by focusing on our breath and then move to mindfully witness sensations and thoughts. Then we will notice the location of the mindful meditator. We'll shift from having the mindful witness be the subject to realize it is an object to our awareness-based effortless mindfulness. Effortless mindfulness is then aware of our breath and body sensations from all around and from within.

1. Sit comfortably and be aware of your body supported on a chair or cushion.

2. Begin to be aware of your felt sense of breathing at one specific area of your body.

3. Notice the feeling of your body in this area as your breath naturally comes and goes.

4. Now, notice sensations in your whole body as sensations come and go.

5. Now, notice thoughts, like mental
   sensations, coming and going.

6. Notice your breath again in this one area
   of your body. Notice the feeling and specific
   location in your body of your breath.

7. Now, be aware of the area you are focusing from.
   Feel local awareness unhook from the focusing
   location and open up into the space all around.

8. Open to the space that is aware of the location
   you were focusing from. Open awareness back and
   out until you are aware *of* spacious awareness.

9. Now, be aware *from* spacious awake awareness
   of the space, your body sensations, and the
   location of your breathing all at once.

10. Feel that you are aware from the spacious
    and pervasive awareness that is effortlessly
    aware of thoughts, feelings, and sensations
    like a seamless ocean of awareness arising as
    the waves of your breath and body. ■

GLIMPSE **Lovingkindness and
Compassion Are Already Here**

Take a few minutes now to experience how you can discover that
lovingkindness and compassion are already here.

1. Sit comfortably, eyes open or closed, and
   be aware of all your senses. Notice the
   activity of thinking in your head.

2. Begin by unhooking local awareness from thoughts in your head. Let local awareness move down to know your jaw from within your jaw. Then feel local awareness move down below your neck. Sense the awareness, aliveness, and space directly from within your body.

3. Become familiar with this direct knowing using local awareness, which is neither looking down from your head nor going back up to your thoughts to know.

4. Feel the awareness and aliveness together as awareness-energy: rest without going to sleep and stay aware without going to thought to know.

5. Feel that awareness can know both the awareness and aliveness from within your body.

6. Notice a feeling of an open-hearted awareness from within the space in the center of your body.

7. Feel as if you have relocated knowing from thinking in your head to this embodied heart-mind within you, which you are now aware from.

8. Notice that you can invite and welcome any thoughts and emotions into the space of your heart-mind, so you can remain at home in open-hearted awareness and have information from the office of your head come to you as if by Wi-Fi.

9. Feel the sense of effortless ease, well-being, and "okay-ness" when you are here now.

10. Notice if there is a subtle sense of joy, tenderness, lovingkindness, bliss, or compassion naturally arising

from here. Sense this natural lovingkindness nourishing every cell in your body and beginning to open outward to everyone and everything all around.

11. Be here now, having dropped your center from head to heart, so you can look out from the eyes of your heart-mind and see how everything looks and feels. Join with the natural lovingkindness and allow it to radiate outward. Feel how your deepest intention has always been for all beings to be well and happy. May all beings be free of suffering and experience naturally interconnected love. ■

GLIMPSE **Embodiment Scan**

Those who have taken a yoga class or a mindfulness-based stress reduction (MBSR) course will likely have done a body scan meditation. This embodiment scan practice is similar, but you are not scanning your body from your everyday mind using attention. This is a "nondual body scan." In this glimpse, we're going to have local awareness unhook from thinking and then drop to know and experience your entire body directly from within and then open to discover the safety of being boundlessly embodied. This is a good practice for helping you wake up from the limitations of your small mind. You may also find that this is a good practice to help you fall asleep at night.

1. Begin by finding a comfortable way of sitting or lying down. Notice the feeling of your breath in your body.

2. Now, shift your awareness to notice the location of where you are focusing from.

3. Next, let local awareness unhook from this focusing location and begin to move down,

feeling its way down through your face to feel
and know your jaw directly from within.

4. Be aware of not looking down from your head to your
body. Notice what it is like when local awareness begins
to know and feel your body directly from within.

5. Feel local awareness move down to sense your neck
from within. Then feel local awareness begin to expand
to include feeling your shoulders, arms, and hands
and then further expand to be aware directly from
within your chest, upper back, belly, and lower back.

6. Allow local awareness to remain aware from within
your upper body and continue moving downward
to include your hips, pelvis, thighs, legs, and
feet, knowing them directly from within.

7. Allow local awareness to be aware of your entire
body from head to toe from within.

8. As your awareness moves down the length of
your body, notice the releasing of holding and a
deep relaxation. Be aware of the space, awareness,
contact, and effervescent aliveness of the experience
of knowing your body directly from within.

9. Feel your body from the awake awareness within as
a field of effervescent energy. Notice the awareness
and energy are mingled as both your soft body and a
boundless quality that begins to open outward. Feel
how energy and movement are happening equally
outside and within and that awake awareness is
aware simultaneously from outside and within.

10. Feel your breath happening by itself like waves in the ocean.
    Feel that awake awareness is also happening by itself.

11. Notice that awareness extends beyond your
    body to notice the space in the room and the
    awareness-energy as an interconnected dynamic
    field subtly connected to everything and everybody
    while feeling embodied here and now.

12. Enjoy the feeling of the natural, boundless
    freedom and awareness-energy embodied.

13. Rest in the fullness of interconnected embodiment. ■

Once you've gotten a feel for effortless mindfulness—unhooking and glimpsing—you can begin to apply the skills in your everyday life, such as working with different kinds of suffering. In the next chapter, we will explore how to relate to physical pain using effortless mindfulness.

4

Effortless Mindfulness Pain Relief

One winter, I was having a wonderful time sledding with my nephew. On one downhill run, we hit a big bump, and my nephew flew into the air and off to one side. I reached for him and pulled him onto the sled as we hit the next bump. That's when I felt a sharp pain in the lower right side of my back; I'd twisted it. It felt as if I were being stabbed by knives that shot a fiery agony down my lower back to my knee. I hobbled around for months as if I were dragging a wooden leg, trying to not aggravate my injury. Sometimes the pain was pins-and-needles dull, and sometimes it was intense, but it was a constant, chronic condition.

Over the next few months, I visited all kinds of doctors, chiropractors, and acupuncturists seeking relief. The diagnosis was sciatica, which is a compression of the sciatic nerve in the upper leg and lower back. I went to my primary care physician, who told me he had suffered from sciatica since he had hurt his back in the Korean War! He said, "There's nothing you can do about it except take some pressure off it. I can give you some medication if you'd like, but the pain will never completely go away. You can do some stretches, but you'll just have to learn to live with it." I chose to not take any pain medication, and I tried some alternative treatments, including deliberate mindfulness, that gave occasional relief, but the pain remained chronic.

At that point in my life, thanks to effortless mindfulness, I had experienced enough of a shift of awareness that I wasn't experiencing much emotional suffering about the pain, but this did not eliminate the continual physical pain. I trusted that all was well and relied on a more deliberate mindfulness approach of observing and not judging unpleasant sensations or feelings, so as not to add more mental suffering to the physical pain. Deliberate mindfulness is helpful with pain because it allows us to separate the objective sensory experience of pain from the more subjective judgments we attach to pain, which color the way we experience it.

While being able to step back and observe the pain from the outside was a great teaching of deliberate mindfulness, it was, unfortunately, not enough to relieve my chronic pain. I learned to accept the pain as it continued and thought that that was good enough, seeing that pain is a part of human life, with no way around it. But then I became curious: could effortless mindfulness treat physical pain the same way that it treated mental and emotional pain?

That's when I began experimenting, and I had a remarkable discovery: the healing power of awake awareness can be applied to pain in the body as well as to the mind. I have found local awareness has an intelligence that can move directly within the signal of pain, to its source, to see what is true. Then, the pain signal goes to the background intelligence of awake awareness.

What Is Pain?

Pain is a normal part of human life. And pain hurts. Although pain feels like a threat, pain is not attacking us. Pain is designed to help us survive. Pain and pleasure are signals. Pain is a signal that something is out of balance in your emotional, mental, spiritual, or physical life and that something needs attention. It is meant to be unpleasant, for a good reason: to bring our attention to a potentially dangerous situation until the issue is treated. The sharp, unpleasant signal is designed that way to make sure we drop everything else and attend to the situation immediately. When pain continues unabated after our best healthy efforts to tend to it in a physical way, we look for ways of stopping it, reducing it, or escaping it in any way we can.

For example, if you're walking barefoot, thoroughly engaged in a conversation with a friend, and you step on a piece of wood and get a splinter, the strong unpleasant pain signal is meant to get you to immediately stop all other interests and attend to the wound. If you had a sharp piece of wood in your foot and it didn't cause pain, you might not bother to take it out, resulting in infection or worse. Once you take care of the immediate problem, or source, the nature of pain is to eventually go away. Pain by itself is not an entity or an enemy that has any motivation of hurting you. It is an important survival mechanism of our body—a communication tool.

By way of our senses, we have contact with experience in and outside of our body that tends to feel either pleasant, unpleasant, or neutral. We tend to like pleasant sensations, which leads to craving what we like and trying to get more pleasure, and we tend to dislike unpleasant sensations, which leads to rejecting what we don't like. When that strong craving or rejection happens, there is a contraction of our greater sense of self into a specific identity of "craver" or "rejecter": we configure our consciousness into a "me" that is a "thinker" or "manager" that has a strategy to get its goals and desires met and believes that that strategy is real and right. Craving and rejection are a normal part of our physical survival, like craving food when we're hungry, but they also become our primary source of suffering when they become our identity.

Rather than reacting to the pain, we must treat the underlying condition that is causing pain in order for it to subside. It is important to first check out the cause of the pain in every way possible so as not to ignore, overlook, or deny a potentially dangerous condition. In some types of chronic pain that we know the cause of, like arthritis or sciatica, the nerve signal system is alerting us of an issue, but there's no splinter to be removed from our back or foot. If we've attended to all the medical and alternative diagnoses and treatments, and the pain still persists, we still have the opportunity to learn some approaches using our own consciousness to relate to pain differently. Effortless mindfulness is a wonderful approach that does not in any way attempt to replace or deny diagnosing the cause of pain and working to cure it through any and all means. I am simply sharing this practice as a suggestion of what can be done in conjunction with any medical treatment.

With effortless mindfulness, we can learn to become *present with the unpleasant*—an important skill that we often avoid learning until we experience inescapable pain. We may already have experienced, through effortless mindfulness, how chattering thoughts recede into background awareness or can be met by open-hearted awareness. The great news is that we can do this with pain signals as well! They can become like thoughts and go into the background of awake awareness. When the pain signals recede to the background or significantly lessen, we no longer have to suffer silently or try to escape the pain through behaviors of shutting down, numbing, addiction, or acting out. By changing how we relate to pain, we can find a doorway to a freedom that allows us to respond to pain from courage and intimacy. We can learn to be present with the unpleasant, remain sensitive without being defensive, and be responsive but not reactive.

When the intelligence of awake awareness knows directly that there is no immediate danger, the pain signal can go into the background. In my own experience with back pain, the pain no longer needed to send a message from my back to my brain to signify "Danger!" or "Check this out!" When I allowed awake awareness to experience itself as awareness-energy and embrace and eventually recognize that my pain was not separate from my intelligent awareness, it put an end to any resistance and secondary suffering. When this happened, the pain energy became effervescent; it gave me a strangely warm and blissful feeling. Because I could work with the pain through my awareness in this way, I came to understand that the sciatic pain signal was not because of a ripped muscle or cut tissue or knife in my back (even though it felt like that at times). It was simply a signal to get me to notice the situation, which was not related to a real threat.

Within a week of starting to experiment using effortless mindfulness, the pain abated, and by the end of the second week, it was at worst an occasional dull ache, like a sore muscle. It has not returned as a chronic condition to this day! I may get a twinge in my back occasionally if I twist suddenly, but even that does not stay long. The other unique change is that pain does not shoot up to my head; I feel it only in my lower back area. This method has not only relieved my own chronic pain, but has worked for many of my clients and students as well. Once local awareness meets and acknowledges the pain directly, most people report reduction in their experience of pain from around an 8 (on a pain scale of 1 to 10) to a dull 2.

Though many of us are not taught this, being sensitive and vulnerable is one of the most beautiful dimensions of human life. However, if we are sensitive, we are exposed to pleasure and pain on the physical, mental, spiritual, and emotional levels. If our best option of treating pain is to defend ourselves by becoming less sensitive, we will feel less pain but also less pleasure and less fullness of life. The interesting process of effortless mindfulness is to become *more* vulnerable and *more* sensitive by opening to a subtler, vaster, more embodied dimension of consciousness that also has more courage and support. This is helpful for all levels of suffering and pain, while at the same time, each type of pain may need to be met with a slightly different approach. The good thing is that the natural intelligence and intuition that are available to us as we shift into open-hearted awareness will give us good clues as to how to meet our particular type of pain in the way that matches our unique system.

I have received many emails and reports at retreats from students who have experienced pain relief from this practice. Not only have they applied it to sciatica and arthritis, but to menstrual cramps, painful recovery after surgery, and other causes of short-term and chronic pain. Here is a report of the usefulness of effortless mindfulness from one student who had lived with chronic pain for many years due to surgery that affected the nerves in his neck:

> Loch's simple but intensive approach to awake-
> awareness drew me in instantly. Here was a practice
> that transported me to a place both deep within and
> way outside my body. Once I learned those exercises,
> those "small glimpses, many times," I realized on
> the spot that first day that without even trying,
> without knowing what would be the case, my pain
> dissipated. I know what it is like to be pain-free, if

even for a little while, each day. It is not something I set out to do, or something I thought I would ever experience. But it's a beautiful side effect of the awake-awareness experience, and the path to open-hearted awareness.

Local Awareness Is the Key to Pain Relief

The key to being able to do this effortless mindfulness pain-relief method is to distinguish local awareness from attention. Let's review the difference with these experiential glimpses so that we get a feel of local awareness.

GLIMPSE   **Experiencing Attention**

1. Look at one of your hands. Now move that hand out of your vision and bring your attention to that hand. Try to continue applying your attention there for a short while.

2. What was your experience of attention like? ∎

Initially, when you use attention to focus, you may feel that your head (where your brain and eyes are located) is your central place of perceiving. When you bring your attention to your hand, does it feel like "you" are in your head, looking down at your hand? Or does it seem as if "you" are shining a flashlight from your head to your hand? Or do you feel connected, as if a telephone cable is running from your head to your hand and sending signals back and forth? Do you feel how attention can wander? Are you able to feel that maintaining attention is a continuous process of remembering and forgetting?

GLIMPSE **Experiencing Local Awareness**

Now that we've experienced attention, let's see how local awareness differs. In order to experience local awareness, you need to unhook local awareness from thought and know your hand directly from within. Try this for yourself now:

1. Unhook local awareness from thought and let local awareness begin to move down through your neck and know your shoulder from within.

2. Slowly move local awareness like a knowing, invisible bubble down your arm into your elbow. Feel the awareness of space and sensation directly from within.

3. Continue to let local awareness move down your forearm until it feels your hand from within.

4. Experience this new type of knowing that is happening directly, from within your hand.

5. Notice that when awareness knows your hand from within, it does not refer to a mental image of your hand. It feels the space and aliveness of the sensations, so there is not a clear boundary of inside and out. ■

Notice the way in which local awareness knows your body directly from within. Once local awareness has unhooked, thought is no longer the primary mode of knowing, yet thought is available as needed. If you do not reference a memory or image of your hand, your experience of your hand shifts into direct knowing. Direct knowing is spacious, alive, and much more fluid in feeling than attention.

You've just experienced how local awareness moves from thinking in your head to being able to directly know from within your hand. Now you can begin to get a sense of the feeling of local awareness unhooking and moving to any area where you are experiencing a pain signal. The important thing here is feeling how local awareness moves and knows directly from within.

GLIMPSE **Effortless Mindfulness Pain-Relief Method**

Here is a mindful glimpse to work with physical pain. Many people have found, with this approach, that their experience of pain and discomfort can change so that suffering is dramatically reduced.

Before you begin, make sure that a medical professional has evaluated your condition. As you practice, don't try to make a heroic effort. Instead, the key is simply this: instead of trying to move away from the pain or finding that you've automatically done so, learn to shift your local awareness to discover the awake awareness that's already with and within the pain. A good metaphor is that the pain is continuously calling the operator in your brain. You can make it so that the operator (in this case, local awareness) can actually go down to meet the caller and see what is going on. Since the pain has been directly met, it no longer needs to try to get the operator's attention, and the phone can stop ringing. Through practicing this exercise, see what you can discover and what might change in your relationship with your pain.

1. Begin by becoming aware of your body, and then notice the area where you feel pain. Notice the qualities of the specific area and its borders—where the pain begins and ends.

2. Notice the area just outside the borders of the pain. Now, notice the space between this area of pain and the location in your head where you're focusing from. Notice the feeling of the pain signal sent from the painful area to your head.

3. Bring your awareness to your head, and instead of looking at the pain from above, as a mindful observer, unhook local awareness from your thinking.

4. Feel local awareness begin to travel internally down to feel your jaw directly from within your jaw.

5. Feel local awareness move to be aware of your throat, knowing your throat directly from within. Now feel local awareness, like a bubble of intelligence, as it continues to move within your body toward the area of your pain.

6. As you do this, feel that you are knowing directly from the local awake awareness that is sensing from within your body. As local awareness moves into the area of pain, allow local awareness to feel gently within the area of pain without referring to thought.

7. Local awake awareness can sense the aliveness, space, and awareness within the atoms of the place of painful signals.

8. Local awareness has traveled to the source of the signal, so there is no distance between the origin of the pain signal and the place where the call is received. Local awareness enters the pain and the space; it gets subtler and subtler. Local awareness joins with the area that's sending the pain signal, and it assesses: *Is there really a threat here now?*

9. Local awareness sees that pain is made of awareness and knows directly that there is no dangerous threat that needs to be constantly monitored. No action, response, or ongoing pain signal is needed to be sent to the brain, as the situation is now clearly seen by the intelligence of awake awareness.

10. Local awareness reaches the pain, meets it, and becomes intimate with it, recognizing that it is not *other*. Let the pain sensations be rerouted to the spacious awake awareness all around your body. Continually responding to the pain

signal is no longer necessary. Local awareness has already responded and is currently within the area of pain. The pain signal can now go into the background, to the field of the intelligence of awake awareness, rather than the small self or small mind. There is a connection to the source of intelligence, a larger field of open-hearted awareness that is embodied and compassionately comforting. ■

In the first part of this book, we've learned how effortless mindfulness is different and complementary to deliberate mindfulness. In part 2, we will go through how to practice effortless mindfulness, step by step, in a variety of new ways, so that you can find your favorite way of accessing this in your daily life to reduce suffering and to discover your optimal mind and your natural joy of being.

Part II
Unfolding

5

_____

Three Hypotheses

I offered an overview of effortless mindfulness and awake awareness in part 1. Now I'll present a set of hypotheses, combined with mindful glimpses, so you can test them out for yourself. I believe the primary role of a teacher is to introduce students to their inner teacher, to encourage curiosity, an open mind, and an open heart. With the tools in part 2, you can compare the way your consciousness has been organized previously to a new way of experiencing perception, knowing, and identity.

Mindful glimpses are an effective method for this purpose because they transcend dogma and offer a scientific approach to waking up and growing up. I have spent much of my life studying contemplative traditions from many cultures. From the beginning, my interest has been to discover the common human principles of accessing awake compassion, joy, and well-being. My intention in this chapter is to present both the obstacles and the approach to living an awakened life in a simple, practical, and contemporary way.

Three Lenses of Consciousness

We can explore a map of consciousness or patterns of experience through three lenses:

- Mind (how we know)

- Self (our sense of identity)

- Awareness (how we perceive)

Exploring effortless mindfulness through these three lenses can support a stable awakened life. Here's a bit more about these three lenses:

- When we look at consciousness through the lens of *mind*, or knowing, we are focused on how we organize and process information. The level of mind we know from changes our way of perceiving and our sense of identity. The most typical way we know how to structure our consciousness is from thinking.

- Regarding *Self*, or identity, we're using the lens of what or who is perceiving. Who or what are we essentially? We can play with shifting from a sense of small self, through an experience of "no-self," and into the interconnected Self. I am using the term *Self* to acknowledge both the ultimate level of what Buddhists call "emptiness" or "no-self" and the relative level of human experience. The level of identity we are operating from will affect our awareness and mind—how we perceive and how we know. These in turn influence our experience of who we are.

- *Awareness*, or perception, refers to how we see things. Awake awareness is the foundation of knowing and identity. However, there are different types of awareness. Depending on what type of awareness we are perceiving from, what we are able to perceive may shift or differ.

Once we understand these three lenses, we can use them to orient ourselves to a new, upgraded view. We can notice a shift in the way we are perceiving, the way we are knowing, and the sense of identity we are relating from. We can get clues about which lens we're looking through based on new ways of discerning subtle differences in our awareness, mind, and sense of Self. In this way, we can find which aspect of consciousness we're experiencing through and untangle the knots of confusion. We can do this by incorporating mindful glimpses into our lives to navigate a new and more profound way of seeing, knowing, and being.

Even though I use terms like *awareness, mind,* and *Self* to describe consciousness, what I am pointing to is beyond words and descriptions. We can understand our consciousness not by talking about it or thinking about it or even labeling it but by wholly seeing, knowing, and being it ourselves.

The result of not upgrading our consciousness is suffering. The Buddhist word for suffering in Sanskrit is *dukkha,* sometimes translated as "perpetual dissatisfaction." When dukkha is addressed by relaxing out of a small mind and small self, we discover the sense of effortless mindfulness, the sense of Ground of Being, the sense of true nature and natural interconnectedness.

Although freedom and well-being are ever present in and as us, we still experience suffering because we are viewing from a limited perspective. This suffering is neither punishment nor caused by something we have done wrong, but instead, it is a current human habit to identify with the limited patterns of consciousness. We are unable to access our natural capacity because we don't even know it's possible or how to awaken.

It's important to remember that the freedom and well-being we seek are already within us. It does not need to be created or developed but simply realized. The process is not so much about adding knowledge as becoming familiar with the new operating system of awareness-based knowing through effortless mindfulness.

There is nothing I say that you need to believe. This is a theory that I continually test based on my own experience, my students' experience, and the reports of the wise folks from every culture and historical time. I can give you the hypotheses, then a set of experiments, and then you will know the results for your Self.

The patterns that contract us into this suffering can be divided into three hypotheses:

> *The Lens of Mind Hypothesis:* We suffer because we are in too small a mind—a fearful, chattering, conceptual mind.

> *Solution:* When we discover the source of mind through effortless mindfulness, we know directly from awake awareness–based heart-mind.

The Lens of Self Hypothesis: We suffer because we are in too small a sense of self—a feeling of a separate, solid "me."

Solution: When we open and move through "no-self" into the interconnected Self, we are able to be with our internal experiences with greater capacity and know our Self as interconnected, safe, and naturally compassionate.

The Lens of Awareness Hypothesis: We suffer because we are in too limited a form of awareness—distracted, narrow, or detached perception.

Solution: When we open our awareness, we are able to perceive from awake awareness and more interconnected dimensions of reality directly.

We can't use limited awareness, small mind, or small self to solve the problems that they are creating. We can't train our small mind to be capable of awakening. Our limited awareness can't know awake awareness. And the small self is not the one who awakens! We will dive in more deeply to the solution for each hypothesis in the sections that follow.

SOLUTION FOR THE LENS OF MIND HYPOTHESIS

We suffer because we are in too small a mind—
a fearful, chattering, conceptual mind.

The solution for this hypothesis is in discovering our awareness-based heart-mind, which is already within us. We learn to shift out of the conceptual small mind that makes us feel alienated, alone, anxious, and fearful and into the support of our heart-mind that is already calm, alert, loving, and wise. While our small mind is changing and formed through genetics and conditioning, heart-mind is unconditioned, invisible, intelligent, and dynamic.

Before going further into our heart-mind, it is important to understand what the conceptual small mind is. Buddhist mind science recognizes the familiar five senses—smell, taste, touch, hearing, and sight—and adds to that a sixth sense: thinking. If thinking is a sense, it is as illogical to say, "I think, therefore I am" as to say, "I hear, therefore I am" or "I taste, therefore I am." Thinking is an important sense for organizing information, but like the other five senses, we cannot know who we are solely through thinking. A baby is conscious before it can use thought, and everyone can see the shining light of "I am" radiated by an infant's presence. It is also true that when we learn to know from heart-mind, we can feel the "am-ness" of our being with or without thought.

If thought is information like sound or taste, and thinking is a sense, then who or what are thoughts appearing to? When thinking appears to itself, thought to thought, it creates a "thinker," which is a self-referencing loop. In Tibetan Buddhism, this looping, or "selfing," is called the "afflictive consciousness" because it creates a limited thought-based sense of self. If, instead, thoughts go to a more spacious mind, they are seen as sense impressions and information. All the senses, including thinking, can be rerouted to appear to awake awareness–based heart-mind.

Rather than organizing our identity as a thinker, with the effortless mindfulness approach, we shift out of the thought-based knowing and into awake awareness–based knowing and ultimately to heart-mind, which is where we can live from. Heart-mind is when awake awareness is embodied, and we can use memory and thought as needed; just as we can drop our hand to our lap when needed, surprisingly, we can drop thought from the foreground to the background, which leads to peace of mind. Rather than the usual habits of going up to look to thought or looking out from a thinker, we simply relax into awake awareness and then know from our heart-mind.

When, through effortless mindfulness, we learn to separate awareness from thinking, we no longer experience thoughts and emotions as the center of who we are. "I am" is no longer thought based, and "I think, therefore I am" becomes "Awareness is awake; therefore, I am."

GLIMPSE **I Am**

Can you let go of referring to thought for a moment and feel just being here now—the feeling of "I am" or being that is independent of "I am this" or "I am that"? ∎

SOLUTION FOR THE LENS OF SELF HYPOTHESIS

We suffer because we are in too small a sense of self—
a feeling of a separate, solid "me."

When we arrive at "Awareness is awake; therefore, I am," we can shift out of small self and live from our vast, interconnected Self. Other names for this Self include *no-self, true nature, unity consciousness,* or *Ground of Being.*

Both ancient wisdom and modern neuroscience agree that there is no location of a separate self in our brain. The brain is a symphony, but no conductor can be found. Living as if there were a small, separate self inside your head is living from a mistaken identity, which is the root of suffering.

From the small self, we are living in too tight a place, not knowing that there is more space available. Too small a mind creates anxiety or depression, too-narrow awareness keeps us seeing with blinders on, and too small a sense of self creates a feeling of separation, loneliness, fear, and isolation. A full, intimate emotional life is too much for this small self because it is a thought-based creation. When operating from a small self, our energy goes down into depression, up into anxiety, or is acted out in emotional outbursts or addiction. We create suffering by trying to solve our problems with only the resources of a small, separate self. The way out of suffering is not to create a smarter small mind, trying to figure it out, or even meditate to calm the small self.

It is not enough to just realize "no-self" and know that the small self is not essentially who we are. The solution begins with realizing that there is already another operating system available and then learning how to upgrade into it. Our interconnected no-self Self, heart-mind, and open-hearted awareness are a new view with more room.

The key to allowing these transitions to fully occur is in resisting the temptation to return to the small conceptual mind for a second opinion to know things once you have learned how to shift into heart-mind. From heart-mind, we move from simply "not knowing" to a "not knowing that knows" things directly, without reflective thought, which is like a continuous intuition. When we rest back into awake awareness, this self-referencing loop dissolves, and then we can feel an embodied awareness-energy interconnected with the world from our naturally awake heart-mind.

The Self (with a capital S) is not a bigger version of the small self, and the small self cannot grow into Self. The small self does not need to be fought, defeated, or erased but needs to retire from its role as the center of identity. In fact, we can thank the small self and give it retirement benefits for working so hard. As we'll see in chapter 7, what we call small self is a group of parts of us, subpersonalities. We can then look at this constellation of small-self system as a way of bringing greater acceptance to our personality.

When I ask people, "Where is your sense of self located?" many tell me it's in their body or upper body, but most say that their normal sense of "me" feels located in their head behind their eyes, looking out at the world and feeling down to their body. They feel enclosed in their head and separate from what they see. With effortless mindfulness, we address the location and formation of consciousness that limits awareness, mind, and Self. We do this not by creating, imagining, or cultivating positive states but by untying knots to reveal the natural condition of our heart-mind and Self. As a student of mine once said, "Everything feels empty and full. I am here and everywhere as if there is no separate self but also things are alive, and I feel like, 'I'm just me.'"

The Buddhist word for emptiness—*sunyata* in Sanskrit—is often misunderstood, but understanding this pointer is essential to realizing effortless mindfulness. Interestingly, the root word for empty—*svi* in Sanskrit—is often described through a metaphor as the invisible life essence within a seed that allows it to grow into a tree. It's not absence but is the dynamic quality of awareness-energy.

Emptiness does not mean that you are totally absent of a small self on the relative level. Emptiness means that everything is empty of a separate, independent existence. For example, a flower is not a flower without its connection to water, to air, to sun, and to earth. Realizing emptiness helps relieve the suffering caused by the mental habit of a small, separate sense of self. This limited mental pattern of small self is attempting to relieve suffering by trying to be both independent and connected. Instead, the pointer of emptiness is actually saying that we are already interdependent or interconnected. From deliberate mindfulness, we have insight into the absence of a separate, solid self. With the experience of effortless mindfulness, it was a great revelation to me when I realized that the simplest and best definition of emptiness is "interconnectedness."

True well-being, the relief of suffering, is not just based on belief or positive thinking but comes from the core realization of interconnected Self, in which we directly experience the reality that we and others are not separate. No matter what difficulties we experience and what beliefs we may have, our true no-self Self is always here to help us come back into perspective, compassion, and wholeness.

GLIMPSE **Who Is Aware Now?**

If there is no need to create a solid, separate self, what or who is aware now? ■

SOLUTION FOR THE LENS OF AWARENESS HYPOTHESIS

We suffer because we are in too limited a form of awareness—
distracted, narrow, or detached perception.

Opening our lens of awareness leads to seeing more clearly and feeling more connected. One significant difference between deliberate and effortless mindfulness is the type of awareness each uses. In this section, we can explore eight distinct types of awareness related to deliberate and effortless mindfulness that will help us discover open-hearted awareness to help us live an awakened life.

The first four types of awareness related to small mind, small self, and deliberate mindfulness are:

1. Attention

2. Self-awareness

3. Subtle energy awareness

4. Mindful awareness

These are followed by four types of awareness that are related to awareness-based mind, Self, and effortless mindfulness:

5. Awake awareness

6. Local awake awareness

7. Awake awareness-energy

8. Open-hearted awareness

GLIMPSE **Looking from Awareness**

When you look at awareness now, does it have a limited shape, size, location, or color? When you look from awareness, is there a center from which you are looking, or is everything interconnected? ∎

In the following sections, we'll look more closely at each of the eight types of awareness.

TYPE ONE   Attention

Attention is the ability to concentrate, focus, and be cognizant of something from our everyday mind so that we can function in our daily activities. As mentioned, the *Merriam-Webster* definition of *attention* is "the act or state of applying the mind to something."[1] Applying the mind is the experience of being a subject located in your small mind, perceiving an object (even a part of your own body) located elsewhere. Attention is related to using our small mind.

TYPE TWO   Self-Awareness

Self-awareness is a psychological term referring to self-reflection and the ability to split off thought to create an observer of one's thoughts, individuality, and behaviors. This unique form of a human being's awareness develops in children when they are between one and two-and-a-half years old, when they begin to recognize themselves as separate individuals from their caretakers. This is when they begin to use the pronouns *I*, *me*, and *mine*. However, it's not the naming of oneself as a separate person that causes a separate sense of self. Self-awareness, which is one of humanity's greatest strengths, leads to the creation of a small self when we split our thinking into two parts. Self-awareness becomes the center of the separate small self that feels like "me." Self-awareness is aware from a manager part (which we'll explore in chapter 7), sometimes called "ego identity."

TYPE THREE   Subtle Energy Awareness

There are two types of subtle energy awareness. The first is internal, which is experienced as energy in and around the body as well as within (like your emotional body, chakra system, chi, prana, central channel in front of your spine, and inner body presence). The second is external, in our environment, such as other people, groups, physical spaces, nature, emotions, objects, and subtle realms often called psychic or spiritual. Subtle energy awareness is a normal human ability to internally and externally feel or perceive people, spaces, and things.

I include this second type of subtle energy awareness of people, places, things, and other dimensions because it has historically been omitted from our Western psychological map or dismissed as if it were imagination or projection. Studies on highly sensitive people, mirror neurons, and what Dr. Dan Siegel, professor of psychiatry at UCLA and executive director of the Mindsight Institute, calls "attunement"[2] in interpersonal neurobiology are beginning to validate this category of awareness within the paradigm of scientific materialism. When I ask a group of students, "How many of you have ever walked into a room and felt that someone is upset without looking at their body language?" usually three quarters of them will raise their hands. (It's important to note that without the grounding of awake awareness—type five—many highly sensitive people can get overwhelmed by subtle energy because, without awake awareness, we are still experiencing sensations and events from the view of a small self within a separate physical body.)

TYPE FOUR   **Mindful Awareness**

Mindful awareness is a witnessing awareness that is sourced in the subtle mind. Subtle mind is what we attempt to access in deliberate mindfulness in order to observe the contents of the mind. It is the ability to step back like a detached observer of thoughts, sensations, and feelings. Mindful awareness is aware of the everyday mind and the commenting, planning, judging functions of self-awareness. It is nonjudgmental and neutral—not attached to thought. Mindful awareness is located as a meditative point of view, which some people call "the observing ego." Whereas self-awareness is a layer of the personality that has an agenda, mindful awareness is the subtlest layer of the small self.

Neither attention, self-awareness, subtle energy awareness, nor mindful awareness can know awake awareness. The next four types of awareness are where effortless mindfulness begins. It is important to distinguish awake awareness from the first four types of awareness to continue to wake up and grow up.

TYPE FIVE   **Awake Awareness**

Beginning with awake awareness, the next four types of awareness are related to effortless mindfulness. Awake awareness is not the stuff between you and an object; it is the foundation of who you are and how you know. Awake awareness is natural awareness that is present already, available to all of us without having to be developed or created. Awake awareness is the source from which all kinds of thought, knowing, and intelligence arise. Awake awareness, as the invisible intelligence, knows that it is what everything is essentially made of. One reason we don't usually tap into awake awareness is that we're generally looking out from it. Awake awareness is the source of knowing, the nature of mind. It is prior to thought, what thought is made of, and beyond thought as non-conceptual wisdom, which can use thought when needed. We can only know awake awareness when it has recognized itself.

Effortless mindfulness begins by looking back through the mindful witness to this spacious, already-awake awareness. This is how effortless mindfulness moves past the deliberate mindfulness levels of awareness. Deliberate mindfulness stops at the point of a mindful witness, or perhaps even at the absence of a separate self or at a gap of not-knowing, or at deconstructing the small mind into its component parts and staying within the realm of psychology rather than finding the Self that can assimilate all of the parts. Effortless mindfulness moves beyond into awake awareness, the spacious emptiness that is everything. The shift from deliberate to effortless mindfulness can feel like a step back from everything, but effortless mindfulness isn't about progressively pulling back farther and farther, zooming out like a movie camera. With effortless mindfulness, we turn awake awareness around to discover who or what is behind the camera. When the meditator is looked for with awake awareness, none can be found because when awareness looks back, the location of the mindful witness merges or dissolves. The magic we discover is that there is seeing but without a seer or source of seeing.

TYPE SIX   **Local Awake Awareness**

Local awareness is the dimension of awake awareness that can move from identification with our body, small mind, and small self to awake awareness. It is also how we focus from awake awareness-energy on any task or object. Once we are introduced to local awareness, we don't have to come back to use attention to focus from awake awareness-energy. Local awareness is like another sense that is designed to know awake awareness. It allows us to be both spacious and present, so we don't have to be either limitless or limited.

TYPE SEVEN   Awake Awareness-Energy

As soon as awake awareness moves from knowing itself as awareness to experiencing any energy, form, or appearance, it becomes what I call *awareness-energy*. In this experience of effortless mindfulness, awareness is not separate from energy or appearances. Thoughts, feelings, and sensations are made of awake awareness and known simultaneously from the outside and from within. It is as if the ocean of awareness, with all experiences, including our own body, is waves of awareness-energy. My friend and colleague, the spiritual teacher Adyashanti, put it this way:

> When we perceive ourselves as consciousness, as awareness itself, it is life changing. This is a significant insight, and we can even call it its own kind of awakening—a fundamental shift out of identification with thoughts and feelings to the purely subjective experience of being consciousness or awareness—*but it is not an end point*. It is a midpoint of realization. We still have a fundamental difference between the perceiver and the perceived, between awareness or consciousness and everything that awareness or consciousness is aware of or conscious of. Next come the deeper states of realization, when the perceiver or the witness state collapses and when the perception of subject and object collapses. That is when we find our truth about the nature of our existence.[3]

The movement of viewing from a mindful witness to awake awareness-energy is the "collapse" or unity of subject and object. The view from awareness-energy feels interconnected with what we are aware of, without being identified with anything. Awake awareness-energy experiences directly from all around and within on a felt-sense level, without viewing from a witnessing awareness, without merging back into subtle energy, and without reidentifying with the small self.

At first, awake awareness-energy is experienced as an all-pervasive field of dynamic intelligence and energy. Then the feeling of oneness becomes a unity that has unique expressions and appearances in the field of perception. There is a simultaneous feeling of local embodiment *and* vast openness *and* interconnectedness to all existence. The root word of the word *existence* in Latin—*existere*—means "to come forth, stand out, or emerge." Here, the wave of awareness emerges from the ocean of awareness while still being of it.

In the North India Mahamudra tradition, this stage of realization is called "one taste" because stillness, movement, thought, sensation, and forms are all recognized to be made of awake awareness-energy. When we are experiencing from awake awareness-energy, we are aware of everything we see with our eyes on not just the physical level but also a felt-sense level.

We can experience boundlessness and boundaries, spacious and permeating awareness-energy, and a feeling of being everywhere and nowhere and very much here. Awareness-energy is not in your body; your body is made of this alive awareness. We simultaneously experience a felt-sense of our body from within and all around, and we feel interconnected with everybody. One of my students reported, "I feel like a cat walking: fluid, connected, both soft and strong, without being tight or in my head."

TYPE EIGHT   Open-Hearted Awareness

Open-hearted awareness is aware from heart-mind. With open-hearted awareness, we can welcome all thoughts and emotions, and we recognize the same open-hearted awareness in others. From open-hearted awareness, we feel connected and protected, vulnerable and courageous, and motivated to create and relate. Open-hearted awareness looks from a wisdom-based loving intelligence that feels boundless, interconnected, and fully human.

We begin to notice infinite boundless love as the ground and then notice our true Self as the open-hearted awareness loving presence. This allows us to feel what we need to do to let that safety be felt, to be vulnerable to the deep abiding safety that is always right here. You need do nothing but receive the love and safety. From open-hearted awareness, you are the Self that is receiving, made of, and giving the unconditional love that arises naturally.

GLIMPSE   **Knowing from Open-Hearted Awareness**

Instead of going to thought to know, look to wordless awareness. Pause . . . and notice this awareness is outside and within. Feel the openness as this field of awareness-energy connects with your body and knows from a new location of open-hearted awareness. ■

6

Practicing the Five Foundations
of Effortless Mindfulness

I
n this chapter (a practice book within a book!), I share mindful glimpses for each of the Five Foundations of Effortless Mindfulness we explored in chapter 3:

1. Awareness of awake awareness

2. Awake awareness as aware of itself

3. Awareness from awake awareness-energy

4. Awake awareness-energy embodied

5. Open-hearted awareness

Here, we'll make the shift from simply learning about the Five Foundations to experiencing them directly. I'll explain them in further detail and then present mindful glimpses related to each foundation. You can also record them in your own voice and at your own pace to experience the mindful glimpses directly.

As you begin these mindful glimpses, it's important to remember how they differ from guided meditations. In mindful glimpses, unhooking awareness has to be fast and direct so that awareness can detach from thinking; otherwise, you might simply be using attention. In mindful glimpses, we don't rely on attention, concentration, willpower, imagination, or thought. We move local awareness into awake awareness as if it were air into air. Instead of a pebble being tossed into a pond, it feels like a drop of water merging with a body of water: that's how we move from a small point of view to perceive from awake awareness.

PRACTICES FOR THE FIRST FOUNDATION OF EFFORTLESS MINDFULNESS
Awareness of Awake Awareness

The mindful attention that is employed in deliberate mindfulness to focus on breath and observe thoughts cannot be used to find awake awareness. Here we discover that we can use local awake awareness to become aware of awake awareness. Awake awareness feels crisply clear like a cloudless spring day. It feels open, infinite, silent, alert, and intelligent. Local awareness is hidden within us and can separate out from our thinking mind and expand into spacious awake awareness. To do this, we unhook, detach, disidentify, surrender, open, or relax local awareness from being identified with thought and other parts of us that have been running the show.

Awareness of awake awareness is the first transition that takes us beyond small mind and small self. To feel awareness being aware of itself, to discover its depth and fullness, awareness needs to go completely beyond referencing the body and mind. You will learn to feel the shift so that even if there are thoughts and sensations, awareness aware of itself is primary.

Understanding that spacious awareness is already awake without our help means that we do not have to create it or develop it. All we need to do is to discover how we can know it and then simply surrender, mingle, or plug into that source. The trick to recognizing spacious awareness is to be clear that we have unhooked from the mind and then the body, without spacing out and without referencing some state of energy or imagination either. Through glimpses, we can learn to distinguish being aware of the space in the room from spacious awareness.

We begin awareness of awareness by having local awareness unhook from thinking and identification with other parts of us. Then local awareness can move to other senses and then to space as transitions to awareness of awareness. Try these five mindful glimpses to see which work best for you.

GLIMPSE **Awareness Following the Breath Home**

Try hitching a ride on your breath to help local awareness unhook.

1. Begin by unhooking local awareness from thinking and have it move a short distance from behind your eyes to where your breath contacts your nostrils. As inhalation occurs, let local awareness focus completely on this small area of sensation. As exhalation occurs, sense the breath touching the nostrils as it goes out. Do this for several breaths in a row.

2. With the next in-breath, allow local awareness to ride the air as it moves from your nostrils down your throat and into your chest or belly.

3. Allow local awareness to unhook from the breath and remain with the awake awareness and aliveness below your neck, even as your breath goes back up and out again. Notice local awareness opening to the aliveness and spacious awareness within your body while not returning to your head and thoughts.

4. Let the feeling of your chest or belly rising and falling with each new breath be the place of contact for your awareness to stay interested. Notice your breath, feeling it from within and opening out, letting go and being here and now. Notice the breath happening by itself

as if you are being breathed. Allow the field of awake awareness to effortlessly focus intimately on your breath. Feel the stillness, silence, and peace beyond words.

5. Notice that the breath is happening by itself, just as awake awareness is also happening and knowing by itself from within and all around. ■

OPEN-EYED MEDITATION

To do small glimpses during the day and transition from small glimpses to everyday activity, we will need to learn how to do these with our eyes open. It can be helpful to begin with some retraining of the relationship between our eyes, our small mind, and our small self. We can begin to return our eyes to their natural condition and have the information move to awake awareness.

According to the American Foundation for the Blind, "vision is the product of a complex system of which the eyes are only one part. The processing of visual information—the receipt of visual stimuli through the eyes, its interpretation by various brain centers, and its translation into visual images—has been estimated to involve as much as 40 percent of the brain."[1]

When our eyes are darting around or scanning for a specific threat, we are on alert. Sometimes our attempts to focus ourselves by narrowing our eyes and concentrating can keep our brain in a fixed, task-positive mode. Our goal in this book is to be able to shift to another operating system, the end point of which is open-hearted awareness, in which all our senses and systems—including vision—are functioning in their natural state: open, relaxed, clear, and integrated. To do this, we need to learn how to shift our awareness and live with our eyes open.

Here are some helpful hints for sustaining an open gaze while shifting awareness. Throughout the remainder of the book, as you do different glimpses, these hints should come in handy. You don't necessarily need to experience all of them as I describe them. Use any of the following hints that work for you:

- Relax your eyes and soften your gaze so that your eyesight is not dominant and all your senses are experienced equally.

- Instead of looking through a narrow tunnel of vision or in a pinpointed way at one object, see the forest as well as one tree. Put your pointer fingers together up above your head in front of you and then part them to either side, drawing a big circle in front of your body. Let your gaze open to include the entire circular area all at once so that you are seeing in a more open way.

- Rather than looking at one object, create a diffused view like a soft lens of a camera by looking to the wider scene of what's in front of you.

- Extend one hand in front of you with your palm facing you at the distance you would be looking at a friend's face. Look at your hand and the space around it. Now drop your hand and look at the open space. If your eyes habitually focus on the first object you see, repeat the previous steps until you get a feel for resting your eyes on objectless space.

- Notice that your eyes do not operate like your hands. You do not go out to see something as your hands go out to pick something up. Your eyes work in a similar way as your ears. Just as your ears are receiving sound, light is reflecting off objects and coming into your eyes. What does it feel like when seeing is receiving?

- Rest back as the light comes to your eyes and then goes to open-hearted awareness while all your senses are open. Feel like you are equally aware of all your senses rather than focusing on seeing or thinking as primary.

- Feel like you are receiving light as you soften your eyes while having a wide-open view of the periphery.

GLIMPSE **Awareness of Space**

Local awareness is malleable: it can focus and join with one of
our senses, or it can unhook and move. In this next glimpse, local
awareness can let go and move to be aware of objectless space.

1. Unhook local awareness from thought
   and let it move to focus on hearing the
   sounds coming into one of your ears.

2. Focus neither on who is hearing nor on what is
   heard, but instead just the sensation of hearing.

3. Notice how awareness is able to focus on the
   vibration of sound in this one small area.

4. Now unhook local awareness from hearing and open to
   the space all around in which sound is coming and going.

5. Notice the movement of sounds through space.

6. Now become interested in the objectless space through
   which the sounds are moving. Feel as if local awareness
   has opened and is knowing the space from the space.

7. Notice the effects of awareness of space. ■

GLIMPSE **Awareness of Awareness**

In this glimpse, local awareness moves outward into space and then
discovers spacious awareness. Here, we will let awareness mingle with
space and then become aware of itself. Because our senses tend to
be oriented to the front of our bodies, it might be easier to discover
spacious awareness when focusing on the space at the sides of your
body or the space behind your body.

Now let's have local awareness unhook from thought, notice one of our senses, and discover local awareness aware of spacious awareness.

1. Unhook local awareness from thought and have awareness move to hearing the sounds coming to one of your ears.

2. Don't focus on who is hearing or what is heard, just the sensation of hearing.

3. Notice how local awareness is able to focus on the vibration of sound at one ear.

4. Just as local awareness can focus on a small area, notice how local awareness can now unhook and open into the space in which sound is coming and going.

5. Rather than focusing on the movement of sounds through space, let local awareness rest in the open space.

6. Local awareness opens to space until it discovers that open space is aware.

7. Feel that local awareness is like an air bubble that opens and blends into the air, mingling with the field of spacious awareness that is already aware.

8. Let awareness palpably know and feel itself as spacious awareness, without looking to thought or sensation.

9. Stay with this contentless, timeless, boundless awareness itself. Remain undistracted without effort. Take as long as you need to get a feel for spacious awareness being aware of itself without any physical or mental references. It can be like tuning in to a radio station of silent pure awareness. Only the knowing from awake awareness can know when you're there.

10. Relax into abiding as this field aware of itself without subject or object for a minute or two.

11. Notice the moving thoughts and then notice stillness. Now rest as awareness of stillness and movement that is silent, thought-free, timeless, boundless, contentless, yet fully alert and aware.

12. Once awake awareness is primary, notice that awake awareness is spontaneously aware of itself, by itself, as itself without any effort. ■

THE FIRST YOU-TURN

Through the next, and final, glimpse in the first foundation of effortless mindfulness, we'll explore how awareness is normally hidden in the background, identified with thought, or misunderstood to be a way of perceiving the things around us. In many meditation systems, awareness, attention, and consciousness are treated as if they're the same. In Western psychology, and even in our common speech, we often use the words *aware* and *conscious* as if they mean the same thing. For example, "I am aware of what I am reading" and "I am conscious of what I am reading." We also use *awareness* and *attention* interchangeably, such as when we say, "Bring your attention to what you're hearing" or "Bring your awareness to what you're hearing." When we conflate these terms, we are regarding awareness as a limited type of consciousness that is "between" self, as the subject, and an object, as in "I am aware of that cup." In this case, awareness is the link between you—the one who is looking—and the cup, which is the object being seen.

Awake awareness is different from attention or consciousness. Awake awareness is not the intermediary between you and an object; it is the foundation of who you are and how you know. Our current sense of "I" is constructed around self-reflective thinking, so when we think we are something smaller than awareness itself, awareness can get caught in the middle and reduced to a function or tool of the mind and identity.

Currently, awareness does not feel like the foundation of who I am but instead feels like it's in the middle: "I am aware of seeing the cup." Here, we are acting as if awareness were a functional tool of "I," as something that connects me and objects around me (that are perceived as outside of me): "I am → aware of → seeing the cup." Let's look more closely at this process:

- "I" is a pattern of thought—small mind—that takes itself to be the subject.

- "Am" is currently connected to the "I" of small self instead of awake awareness.

- Awake awareness is reduced to being seen simply as "attention," a tool for focusing. It's considered to be an intermediary process rather than the foundation of who I am.

- "Seeing" is the particular sense that is being used in this example.

- "The cup" is the object of focus—the seen.

When local awareness does a "you-turn" and looks back, it sees through the small sense of self and discovers that awake awareness is now where "I am" is located.

The you-turn reverses the process of perception: Awake awareness can move from being a mode of perception between you and something you observe to instead turning around and looking back through the mental pattern of "I" to find itself. Awake awareness becomes the primary location of observing. The "am" is no longer located within thinking but is now directly experienced as awake awareness aware of itself, your body, and the cup.

GLIMPSE **The You-Turn**

Find an object, such as a cup, a pen, or even this book, place it in front of you, and try doing the you-turn.

1. Notice that you are aware of the object in front of you. Notice the feeling of going out from your body toward the object.

2. Now let local awareness turn back to the space between you and the object.

3. Let local awareness rest back to the space between your eyes.

4. Let local awareness rest back to the space between your ears.

5. Now let awareness rest back behind your body into the space behind.

6. As local awareness rests back behind your body, notice that spacious awake awareness is already aware and feeling forward through your body and to the object without using concentration or attention.

7. Just see and be. Experience awareness of awareness as spacious and pervasive. ■

PRACTICES FOR THE SECOND FOUNDATION
OF EFFORTLESS MINDFULNESS

Awake Awareness as Aware of Itself

As local awareness becomes aware of spacious awareness, it begins to recognize itself. Local awareness and spacious awareness then unite, realizing they have always been united, like an air bubble bursting into air. From this perspective, there is no longer a subject knowing an object; there is just awake awareness knowing itself. Awake awareness knows itself by *being* itself.

Awake awareness is infinite, invisible, inherent, and most importantly, intelligent. However, what it knows has no conceptual information. There is a new kind of direct knowing that starts with not-knowing, which becomes a not-knowing that *knows*.

This awareness of awareness is what gives us the opportunity to experience essential freedom, the first glimpse of who we essentially are: boundless ground that needs nothing and can't be hurt by anything. It can feel like such a relief from difficulties in life that one of my students who had this experience asked, "Is this legal?"

Importantly, we can't live exclusively in a field of awake awareness because it is not possible to function in the physical world from a perspective and Self that is mainly nonphysical. Furthermore, we don't want to get stranded at a waystation, halfway home. That said, the new way of experiencing ourselves that we'll be coming into as we glimpse the following foundations of effortless mindfulness requires the direct experience of this stage of awareness knowing awareness.

One way to check if we are in the second foundation of effortless mindfulness is to inquire: "Am I aware of spacious awareness, or is spacious awareness aware of itself?" Be with this inquiry and experiment with it until you can start feeling a shift in your perspective so that awareness is now resting as itself. In Tibetan Buddhism, the first foundation, awareness of awareness, would be considered the stage of *recognition*, and the second foundation, awake awareness aware of itself, would be known as *realization*. You are not the one experiencing awake awareness; you are that. It is important to have this shift of subject-object, this shift in realizing who is "you." This is a shift out of self-center and identity. If you can abide as awareness of itself—contentless, timeless, boundless, knowing—for even three seconds to three minutes, that experience can shift you into realization. To be free of our thought-based operating system, we just need to realize ourselves as spacious awareness until it becomes our new boundless ground.

GLIMPSE **Mind, the Gap**

This glimpse is about finding awake awareness in the gap between thoughts. You may be familiar with a meditation practice in which you repeat a word or a sacred phrase, known as a mantra. Instead, in this glimpse you focus not on the word or its meaning but on the space—and awareness—between the words. Give your thinking mind the simple task of repeating a word to occupy it while you become aware of the gaps between your thoughts. As you explore the presence of awareness in this space, you may begin to notice that awake awareness is already aware.

1. Begin by silently and slowly repeating in your mind, "Blah," with some space in between. "Blah . . . blah . . . blah." Allow the word *blah* to float through the space of your mind like a feather. Don't create any other thoughts or be interested in any thoughts that arise. Let *blah* occupy all the interest and activity of thinking.

2. Begin to be aware of the thought-free space between the words: "Blah" . . . space . . . "blah" . . . space . . . "blah" . . . space.

3. Next, become more interested in the quality of the space between the words. See if you notice that the space is not just a gap but that the space itself is aware. "Blah" . . . aware space . . . "blah" . . . aware space . . . "blah" . . . aware space.

4. Feel the spacious awareness in between the words and all around them as a field of awake awareness in which the word *blah* and other thoughts now appear. Feel your mind not as a solid thing but as clear, open, and aware.

5. Stop saying "blah" to yourself and just feel into the space you have been noticing. Feel and be this awareness that is awake and alert. Notice that you don't need

to go to thought to be aware. Notice the ease and
natural welcoming of all experiences that arise.

While doing this practice, you may notice that there are two
types of space. One is physical, such as the space in the room you
are in—the absence of objects and content. In art, this is called
"negative space"—the space between things. The other type of space
is presence, which is aware and awake. It is not just empty—it is a
positive space. Awake awareness is alive and conscious.

Whether there are thoughts or no thoughts on the screen of your
mind, there is a background knowing that can move to the foreground.
This silent, spacious awake awareness doesn't use thought to look to
other thoughts to confirm that you know what you know. ■

GLIMPSE **Awareness Yoga**

In yoga training, one is taught how to move the body to feel renewed,
refreshed, balanced, and unified. Here, we will learn to move
awareness for the same purposes. Use these four pointers one at a
time to shift your view, pausing in between to experience what they
point to. Instead of trying to understand the meaning of each pointer,
just be curious. Let your awareness look. Repeat each one as many
times as you like. You can say these phrases with your eyes open or
closed, as you prefer. The important thing is to shift awareness to
look and to *feel* where you're looking from after you shift.

1. Look from awareness and say to yourself:
   I am curious what the next thought will be.

2. Now look from awareness to experience the space
   through which thoughts and sounds are moving.

3. Now look from awareness to see: *What is
   aware of space and moving thoughts?*

4. Now look from awareness and rest as the awake awareness that is aware of itself, by itself, as itself. ■

GLIMPSE **Infinite No-Self**

In this practice, we shift away from the mindful witness and any tendency to contract into a point of view. The feeling of being a self is the feeling of being an observer with a particular location. No-self is the realization that we are everywhere, nowhere, and *here*. We can let go of the tendency to construct a subject-versus-object view or holding on to positive qualities that arise—like bliss, clarity, and non-thought. We no longer look from a particular location of the ego, the meditator, or sky-like spacious awareness. When we shift away from the self-location, we can let everything be as it is, and paradoxically, we will feel ordinary in an open-hearted way.

Here, we will check for any remnant of the location of an ego, meditator, or "small self" viewpoint so awake awareness can become aware of itself.

1. As you take the next breath, focus on the feeling of breath moving in your body. Unhook local awareness from the focusing and have it search your entire body-mind from head to toe to see if a self as an object or subject can be found. Allow the awareness to scan quickly and thoroughly until nothing is found.

2. Upon not finding a "self" located in any one place or looking from any one place, notice how awake awareness and aliveness are free and unconfined and seamlessly permeating.

3. Notice that the field of open and empty awareness is aware of itself, by itself, as itself. The awake field is infinitely aware from everywhere, interconnected to everything. The ocean of awareness knows all waves from inside the wave.

4. Feel that there is no boundary, no center, and yet observing is occurring with no observer.

5. Notice the arising of your human body out of formless awake awareness, moment to moment.

6. Notice the quality of the Now, where everything is here all at once.

7. Let everything be as it is, ordinary and free. ■

PRACTICES FOR THE THIRD FOUNDATION
OF EFFORTLESS MINDFULNESS

Awareness from Awake Awareness-Energy

The way that I experience, practice, and teach this third foundation has changed in some ways since I wrote my first book, *Shift into Freedom*. My experience and thus description of this foundation has been positively influenced by my colleague, with whom I co-teach, Anna-Lisa Adelberg, director of Luminous Awareness Institute. She helped experientially clarify this important phase of awareness-energy, and I am able to describe and invite others into it in more depth now.

Anna-Lisa uses a reference to "Goldilocks and the Three Bears" to explain the feeling of awake awareness-energy: "When you're too identified with your experience, then it feels like 'porridge too hot.' When you are too disidentified as a detached witness, it feels like 'porridge too cold.' When you shift into the view from awake awareness-energy, it feels like 'porridge just right.'" When we are truly looking from awake awareness-energy, we are not a separate, detached witness of objects moving through space. Everything that appears is interconnected energetic aliveness because the realization is that energy is made of awake awareness. The feeling is like the ocean of awareness is arising as this wave of my body and mind, which are not separate from the awake field of awareness-energy.

The first two radical shifts of perspective are moving out of small self and small mind to then being located as spacious awake awareness.

This next shift is to experience everything as an interconnected, dynamic field of awareness-energy. An important distinction that is not often made is that the view from any no-self, open-sky witness that experiences thoughts and appearances as if they were birds and clouds moving through the sky is a meditation state rather than awareness-energy. When you are aware from awareness-energy, you are connected with every experience rather than detached from them. Certainly, on the visual and physical, conventional level, we experience things as separate objects. However, we are talking about a simultaneous perception of interconnectedness on the most essential level, which has been called "emptiness-appearance."

We can remain effortlessly focused in awake-energy because its foundation is awareness-energy rather than a changing mind or a detached mindful witness. From here, we can practice effortless mindfulness embodied, as we observe thoughts, sensations, feelings, and mind objects. We see that thoughts are not who we are, but we also have the insight that they are made of awareness, and there is no need to get rid of them.

We learn to trust that knowing is happening from the intelligence of awareness-energy, and we no longer need to return to conceptual thinking for a second opinion or to create a "thinker." Once this important foundation is established, we can move to the new, daily operating system of open-hearted awareness in the world.

This is important because many people I meet have a "waking up" experience but lapse back into a mindful witness, detached observer, or big-sky mind. Our interest is not waking up from our sense of self into separation from daily life but instead waking *into* a fully alive human life. The stage of awake-energy is an integration in which we discover that energy is made of awareness, so we can feel embodied and alive without getting stuck in a detached witness or becoming reidentified. Awareness-energy is often called "simultaneous mind" or the stage of "one taste" in the Mahamudra tradition because all unique appearances have the same essential flavor of awake awareness. This may seem esoteric at first, but give it a try, and you'll find that awareness-energy leads to a sense of feeling supported and of well-being.

Here, from the intelligence of awareness-energy, we feel connected with everyone and everything. There is a sense of being simultaneously everywhere, nowhere, and very much here. A sense of being interconnected is a unity feeling that begins to be embodied and grounded in a new sense of safety.

GLIMPSE **Effortless Focus**

Unlike the freedom of awake awareness, when we discover awareness-energy, we feel a unity with everything. When we are looking from awareness-energy, we can focus effortlessly.

1. Begin by taking a nice, easy breath. Notice the sense of thinking happening in your head. Have local awareness unhook from thinking and drop down to feel your jaw from within your jaw. Notice that awareness is not looking up to thought nor stretching attention down. Feel local awareness drop below your neck to an open space within your body where you are directly aware of space, vibration, and awareness.

2. Now open awareness out to the space in the room and become aware of mingling awareness with space. Feel a sense of open space that is silently aware.

3. Now see what it's like to be aware of spacious awake awareness as boundlessly as possible. Notice that this boundless, timeless awareness is aware of itself, by itself, as itself, without any help.

4. Notice that your view is as spacious awake awareness for a moment or two. Feel that when you turn to be aware of anything, you are aware from a field of interconnected, all-pervasive, intelligent awareness-energy.

5. Rather than looking from the sky of spacious awareness, notice the feeling of interconnection with sound, light, and energy on a subtle level. Feel as if everything that arises is made of awake awareness. Feel the unity of awareness-energy as you perceive that you are not separate from anything.

6. From the field of awareness-energy, notice the feeling of your whole body arising like a wave from the ocean of awareness-energy. From here, become interested in one point of contact within your body where your breath is arising at your belly or your chest. Begin to focus on the sensation and movement of your breath in this small area. Once you feel your belly or chest begin to rise, label it "one."

7. Then feel a natural pause at the top of the in-breath. Be aware of awareness-energy from all around and within the pause before the out-breath.

8. Then feel the point of contact with your skin as your breath goes out and label it "two."

9. Feel the pause before the next in-breath and rest in the unity of embodied awareness-energy.

10. Your breath is happening by itself, and awareness-energy is aware by itself without creating a point of view. Continue to focus effortlessly as you label each following breath, in and out, with a number up to thirty.

11. Shift into the view from the intelligence of the all-pervasive awareness-energy as thoughts, sensations, and emotions arise as awareness-energy. Simply allow them to appear and go nowhere even as they change. Notice any tendency to become drawn in by pleasant content or to contract against

unpleasant feelings. Feel your unity with all things, boundless, timeless, and dynamically energetic, while effortlessly focusing on your simple breath. ∎

GLIMPSE **Panoramic Awareness**

There is a Tibetan Buddhist practice called "sky-gazing." You physically go to a place with a wide-open vista, and you become interested in looking at the open space. The exercise moves from being vision based to being awareness based. First you notice the open space in front of you, then within you, and then behind you. This gives you an experience of awareness of awareness.

In this effortless mindfulness glimpse, you will move awareness in a full circle, starting at the front of your body, moving to the sides and then behind you so that you feel a 360-degree panoramic awareness. Then you become aware from awareness-energy back to your thoughts, feelings, sensations, and body.

1. Sit comfortably with your eyes open and look directly in front of you. Allow your eyes to look into space rather than focusing on one particular thing.

2. Without raising your chin, bring your gaze slightly upward, as if you are on a beach, looking at the open sky.

3. Without moving your eyes or head, begin to open local awareness outward to both sides so that your peripheral vision expands slowly and gently.

4. As your peripheral vision widens, allow awareness to continue to open gently around toward the sides of your head.

5. Now allow local awareness to unhook from seeing to become aware of the space at the sides of your head through which sound is coming and going.

6. Continue to open local awareness to the felt sense of space behind your body where sound is moving.

7. Feel the sense of spacious awareness all around.

8. Notice how your view is open in a panoramic way.

9. Open local awareness beyond thought and sensations until it mingles with spacious awake awareness that's already awake by itself. Let awake awareness rest as itself.

10. Inquire: *Am I aware of spacious awareness, or is spacious awareness aware of itself, by itself?*

11. Notice how spacious awake awareness is timeless, contentless, silent, and boundless.

12. As you begin to be aware from the panoramic field of awareness-energy, notice how you are subtly interconnected with sound, light, and movement.

13. Feel the ocean of awareness-energy arising outside and within your body as a wave. Feel the balance of being aware equally outside and within your body.

14. Remain undistracted, without effort.

15. Breathe in and allow a smile to come to your face and then feel spacious and pervasive awareness-energy seamlessly all around and within.

16. Notice how your ears are receiving sound without effort.

17. Notice, in the same way as sound comes to your ears, that light reflects off things and comes to your eyes. Let your vision relax and experience seeing as receiving.

18. Remain undistracted as you feel the awareness-energy equally outside and within and the ability to effortlessly focus on your breath as it arises and passes, moment to moment, in the timeless here and now of seamless awareness-energy. ∎

PRACTICES FOR THE FOURTH FOUNDATION OF EFFORTLESS MINDFULNESS
Awake Awareness-Energy Embodied

In the fourth foundation, we arrive at the Ground of Being. When people first move from all-pervasive awareness-energy to the Ground of Being, which is awareness-energy *embodied*, I ask them, "How does it feel?" Many people say, "It feels grounded." When I ask them, "What is the ground made of?" they look puzzled at first, but then, after a moment, say, "Awareness," "Emptiness," "Nothing," "Everything," "Connection," or "Flow." They go on to describe having a profound feeling of safety, effortlessness, and knowing that all is well, using phrases like, "Nothing can threaten who I am" and "Everything is okay." This is the source and resource of effortless mindfulness.

People's first association with the word *ground* is generally of something physical and solid. Although the ground of your being is not physically solid like the earth under your feet, it is supportive, foundational, and safe. Unlike what you may have imagined your foundation to be, the Ground of Being is made of awareness, safety, interconnectedness, well-being, and flow. The Ground of Being is the meeting place between the boundless ground of awake awareness and your human body and personality. Boundless ground plus human equals human being. Asked about this experience while immersed in it, one of my students reported, "I feel profound well-being, an innocence, and a sense that all is well."

Awake awareness-energy is embodied not just as your body but as an interconnection with every body and every thing. The Ground of Being is experienced not only inside your body but also all around. The new feeling is not that "awareness is in my body" but that your body is arising from awareness. There is a deep restfulness as well as a new motivation to engage in life from a natural flow state.

There is a new sense of nonconceptual knowing that has qualities of non-fear, non-shame, non-worry, non-blame, and non-projection. Our intelligence is no longer caught in an either/or bind. It is an intuitive intelligence. From the Ground of Being, there is a sense of boundlessness, and yet you have more ability to set healthy boundaries.

Until awake awareness is embodied, the small self will activate the nervous system to continue, to no avail, to seek safety for itself. Being is the essential "okay-ness" that is already here. When the nervous system and instincts are connected to this essential "okay-ness," there is a huge sense of relief, deep rest, and well-being from which all thoughts and actions begin to spring. After making a connection with the Ground of Being, one student reported, "I have had anxiety dreams all my life. These ranged from not being prepared for a test to the impending death of members of my family or myself. When I shifted into the Ground of Being for the first time, I stopped having anxiety dreams that night, and now I haven't had one for the last year and a half." When trying to manage their busy, modern lives from small self and small mind, people often experience free-floating anxiety throughout the day. The solution to this is moving to the Ground of Being, which we could call "free-floating well-being." Here is a longer description of the Ground of Being that a student sent to me:

> When I experience the Ground of Being: I am at peace
> with life and accept everything as it is. I don't feel like
> anything needs to change. I already feel comfortable
> and safe, as if I am held by something larger than

myself. I feel my "place in the order of things." I am
interconnected and present, without having to "do"
anything to earn it, keep it that way, or make sure
things are okay. I have that feeling of "nowhere to go
and nothing to do," even though I am still fully capable
of going anywhere and doing anything—in other
words, I am able to move through my everyday life fully
connected from the Ground of Being.

People who learn this foundation of awake awareness-energy
embodied are astounded that they can immediately shift into this
Ground of Being level of awareness-energy while doing everyday activities in a stress-free flow—with their eyes open. The Ground of Being
is the ultimate well-being that is here no matter what difficulties occur
in our daily lives, though it can sometimes be in the background.

In this fourth foundation, we become aware that we are both infinite and finite. It feels like the ocean of awareness-energy is arising as
the wave of a new sense of "me." It's also important to note another
paradox about awareness-energy: in the fourth foundation there is
simultaneously a sense of energy and flow (movement) and of stability (stillness). The stillness is now also present because of the Ground
of Being—the stable fullness, the ground that is everywhere, that you
can relax into and feel safe in, that you can feel in your body. *But
what about the energy?* Many people begin to feel a subtle sense of bliss
arising both within their body and as if the world is alive and spar-
kling. This is the movement, feminine, dancing aliveness that is called
"shakti" in India and "emptiness-bliss" in Tibetan Buddhism. This is a
real and natural quality of this foundation's unfolding that is different
from blissful pleasure that comes and goes.

You may remember that we explored the "flow state" in chapter 1.
It is in this fourth foundation of awareness-energy embodied that you
feel both the ground and the flow state, or that feeling of "being in
the zone." This is the other paradox of the fourth foundation: a new
kind of stillness *and* flow. In this flow state, you're effortlessly moving
around, doing activities in which time slows down; your concept of self

is interconnected with everything around you; and you're embodied and operating from a nonconceptual intelligence that knows just what to do.

GLIMPSE   **Awake Awareness-Energy Embodied**

Experiencing the ground of awareness-energy simultaneously within and around your body can decrease the self-referencing mind-wandering associated with the default-mode network. This type of mind-wandering ceases when the two networks of the inward and the outward focus become synchronized, and we become more present and in our body.

In this practice, we are shifting from a detached witnessing self to embodied awake awareness. Try this mindful glimpse a number of times until you get the feel of the equal balance of awareness outside and within as a continuous field. Once you get this for about three minutes, it seems to break the default mode habit, and most people experience a stable, undistracted flow.

1. Unhook local awareness from thought and have it shift to hearing from one ear.

2. Notice the effect of awareness focused on a small area and simply hearing.

3. Just as the local awareness can focus on a small area, experience local awareness opening to the space outside your body where sound is coming and going.

4. Instead of focusing on what is moving through the space, allow local awareness to become interested in space.

5. Notice the shift from awareness of space to noticing that space is aware. Pause and allow this tuning in to spacious awake awareness to happen clearly.

6. Allow awareness to be aware of itself as a contentless, formless, timeless field of awake awareness. Allow your sense of awake awareness to be boundless.

7. Feel the discovery that you have let go of small self and are now located in this boundless awake awareness. When you turn to be aware from awake awareness, notice that the field of awareness-energy is already connected to everything all around and within your body as an ocean of awareness that is arising as waves of aliveness and sensation.

8. Looking with awareness, inquire: *Where am I aware from?*

9. Feel the unified field that is awareness-energy both outside and within simultaneously.

10. Feel the seamless unity of awareness-energy that has no outside or inside.

11. Without going up to thought, down to sleep, or back into a daydream, stay with the knowing from the field of awareness-energy that is naturally inclusive and undistracted. Feel the movement of sound and breath both outside and inside. Feel that awareness-energy is equally aware seamlessly outside and inside, without having to alternate.

12. Marinate in this effortless mindfulness. ■

GLIMPSE **The Now**

The most classical form of Self-inquiry is to ask, "Who am I?" Adyashanti's teachings help us realize awake awareness as source by asking, "What am I?" Most of the glimpses that I have been presenting have focused on shifting out of the small self and the meditative point of view by asking, "Where am I?" When we transition back from boundless, timeless awake awareness to awake awareness-energy embodied, we begin to feel that the Now is both timeless and able to function with conventional clock time. If we want to learn to be in the Now, we can ask, "When am I?"

Here we can begin to experience the Now with one of the most famous Mahamudra instructions, based on the teachings of the first-century Indian Tantric practitioner and spiritual adept Tilopa, called "Six Points of Tilopa" or "Six Ways of Resting the Mind in Its Natural Condition." It advises:

Don't recall.	Let go of the past.
Don't anticipate.	Let go of what may come in the future.
Don't think.	Let go of what is happening in the present.
Don't examine.	Don't particularize or analyze.
Don't control.	Don't try to make anything happen.
Rest.	Relax naturally, right Now.[2]

The Now is the timeless time of awake awareness that includes the three times of past, present, and future. We can learn not to collapse into identifying with one particular time or state of mind. We can familiarize ourselves with the view from the Now, which experiences everything all at once. Here is a modern version of this to help you experience being in the Now.

1. Right now, let local awareness unhook from thought and drop below your neck.

2. Feel the thoughts that come and go, the tick-tock of each moment appearing and disappearing.

3. Open to the now that doesn't get stuck in any present moment. Feel from timeless, spacious awareness that includes past, present, and future.

4. Be aware as each new present moment arrives and passes.

5. Notice that being fully here and now—from awake awareness—there is no problem with being aware of the past, present, or future.

6. Inquire: *What's here now?*

   Don't go up to refer to thought.

   Don't go down to fall asleep.

   Don't go back to refer to the past.

   Don't go even one moment forward to anticipate the future.

   Don't cling to the passing present moments.

   Don't look out to the world to create a subject-object relationship.

   Don't fall into daydreaming.

7. Feel the magnetic pull forward to the future, the pull back to the past, and the pull to try to hold on to the present.

8. Rest your awareness equally inside and outside. Open to the Now and notice the timeless, continuous field of awareness-energy in which all of these present moments of experience are appearing and disappearing.

9. Let go, relax, and be in the all-at-once-ness of the Now.

10. Without going to thought, what's here now
    when there is no problem to solve? ■

GLIMPSE   **Emotions as Awareness-Energy**

When you start this exercise, bring your awareness within your
body and find any emotion that is there now. You can do this
exercise with any emotion, pleasant or unpleasant, but when you
do this for the first time, please try it with an unpleasant emotion.
If you don't have an unpleasant emotion available, choose the
unpleasant emotion that you encounter most often in your life. If
necessary, you can go to a memory or a recent situation in your
life to bring up an unpleasant emotion. By practicing this, you
will learn that you can feel sad without being sad, anger without
being angry, and more.

1. Find an emotion—fear, anger, or jealousy, for
   instance—and begin by feeling it fully. (I'll use
   sadness as an example in the following steps; you
   can substitute whatever emotion you choose.)

2. Silently say to yourself, "I am sad."

3. Fully experience what it is like to say and feel "I am sad."
   Stay with this experience until you feel it completely.

4. Now, instead of saying, "I *am* sad," take
   a breath and say, "I *feel* sadness."

5. Notice the shift from "I *am*" to "I *feel*." Experience
   this shift and the new feeling of being. From here,
   feel your relationship to the sadness as a feeling.

6. Shift again by saying, "I am *aware* of feeling sadness."

7. Experience *awareness* of feeling sadness fully. Shift into an observing awareness. Notice the different emotional quality that comes from this.

8. Shift again, and silently say "Sadness is welcome."

9. Starting from awareness, experience what welcoming the feeling is like.

10. Feel the awareness-energy embody and embrace the feeling. Notice the different emotional quality that comes from welcoming. Sense the support that welcoming brings.

11. Finally, say, "Awareness and sadness are not separate."

Pause to feel awake awareness around and within you, permeating the emotion fully, but without identifying with the emotion or rejecting it. Feel awareness-energy with emotion fully from within. Feel the awareness, the energetic aliveness, the deep stillness of presence. Notice the feeling of looking out at others and the world from this embodied, connected, open-hearted awareness. ■

PRACTICES FOR THE FIFTH FOUNDATION
OF EFFORTLESS MINDFULNESS

Open-Hearted Awareness

From our experience in the mindful glimpses, we now know awake awareness, which has the pristine clarity of a vast, stunning morning sky. Awareness-energy then reveals the dynamic aliveness of interconnection. The Ground of Being brings the balance of including the rest of the dark night sky, where there is a feeling of stillness deeper than sleep, yet wide awake—a primordial peace. This is the effortless stability we've been seeking. As the Ground of Being becomes more established, the dance of bliss and fabric of love unfold into open-hearted awareness from which we engage in compassionate and creative actions and expression.

We now discover heart-mind and the nonconceptual open-hearted awareness that is the important source of our new way of knowing. From open-hearted awareness, we experience life from our heart and the field of love, which, including all steps before it, still includes spaciousness, embodiment, energy, and ground. We are living from our true essence, our interconnected Self, and we are directly experiencing and being with the content within and around us, whatever it may be. We are settled in the Ground of Being, and we are viewing and acting in the world and in our everyday lives in a state of flow, from our heart-mind.

From open-hearted awareness, we welcome all thoughts and emotions, and we recognize the same awake awareness and heart-essence in others: we see them for their true essence and thus see with acceptance, compassion, gratitude, and love. We have moved from witnessing self to no-self in awake awareness to "seeing from Being," where we feel nothing is missing, and "I"—as open-hearted awareness—cannot be harmed. We are aware of our emotions, patterns of ego-identification, and our subpersonalities arising within us, yet we don't become identified. This ability to remain connected to everything gives us more space and wisdom, more capacity to choose how to respond when emotions, opinions, and thoughts arise. From the support of open-hearted awareness, we can begin to detox repressed emotions and rewire our brain to live from the new operating system. We can focus within or outside our body using local awareness, and compassionate activity becomes our natural expression.

GLIMPSE **Drop from Head to Heart-Mind**

This is moving into effortless heart-mindfulness, when we feel like we've dropped from our head to our heart-mind. It feels like we are spacious and embodied and now literally operating from our heart-mind. But the heart-mind is not our emotional heart; it's not our physical heart; it's not even our heart chakra. It's an intelligence that is called *bodhicitta* or *prajna* in Sanskrit. In the Christian tradition, it's the *oculus cordis*—the eye of the heart.

Take a few minutes now and glimpse open-hearted awareness for yourself. Sit comfortably, eyes open or closed, and simply be aware of all your senses. Notice the activity of thinking in your head.

1. First, unhook local awareness from thoughts in your head. Next, let local awareness move down through your neck and into your chest, and then know—directly—from within your upper body.

2. Become familiar with this direct knowing, which is neither looking down from your head nor going back up to your thoughts.

3. Feel the awareness and aliveness together: rest without going to sleep and stay aware without going to thought to know.

4. Feel that awareness can know both the awareness and aliveness from within your body.

5. Notice your heart-mind, a feeling of open-hearted awareness from within the space in the center of your chest.

6. Feel as if you have relocated from your head to the space of your heart-mind, which you are now aware from.

7. Notice that you can invite and welcome any thoughts and emotions into your heart space, so you can remain at home in your heart-mind and have information from the office of your head come to you as if by Wi-Fi.

8. Be here, receive light with your eyes, and look out from the eyes of open-hearted awareness. ∎

GLIMPSE **"Om Sweet Home" in Your Heart**

Here is a mindful glimpse that begins with making a sound and then feeling the vibration in the middle of your chest. This can be a helpful way to invite awareness to unhook from thinking and know the aliveness and awareness directly by using sound and vibration as support.

1. Place your hand on the middle of your chest. Feel your chest expanding under your hand as your breath comes in and relaxing as your breath goes out. Sing, tone, or chant "om," "amen," "home," or "shalom"—or just "hmm." Focus on the feeling of the vibration in the center of your chest.

2. Unhook local awareness from your thoughts and allow it to be drawn down to the vibration and awareness in the center of your chest. Feel as if your heart-mind is the new home of knowing from awake awareness.

3. Without using thought, become aware of the stillness, vibration, and awareness that is pervasive within, and then open your awareness past your body's boundaries to mingle with the support of spacious awareness all around.

4. Allow the awareness of your heart-mind to know itself and then open to connect to all else as well.

5. Hang out and marinate in this continuous field of aware, loving presence.

6. Know from this open-hearted awareness without going back to your head to know. ■

GLIMPSE **Knowing from Heart-Mind**

The Tibetan Buddhist Tonglen practice is interesting because it's the opposite of some New Age practices such as breathing in positive energy and love and breathing out negative energy and suffering. Tonglen practice is a practice of giving and receiving in which one is instructed to breathe into the heart the suffering of others with the wish to take away their ignorance and pain. Then you breathe out of your heart, sending good feelings, compassion, and happiness to particular people or groups.

This next mindful glimpse is what I call a "nondual giving and receiving" practice. You can do this practice by yourself, sending compassionate energy to someone in your life, or you can do this sitting across from a friend. It is the same as the traditional relative-level Tonglen practice, except that when you breathe into your heart, you don't stop at taking the suffering into your body. Instead, you allow it to continue through your heart space to the support of awake awareness behind your heart. Then you feel the support of awake awareness-energy coming back into your body. Next, you feel the loving awareness-energy go out to another person in front of you and connect to the awake awareness within and behind that person. As you breathe in, you feel their ignorance and suffering coming back to and through your body and back to the support of awake awareness. The key experience could be summarized this way: *Awake awareness has your back. We can learn to receive and give from here.*

Take a few minutes to glimpse open-hearted awareness for yourself.

1. Sit comfortably, eyes open or closed, and simply be aware of all your senses.

2. Notice the activity of thinking in your head.

3. Now unhook local awareness from thoughts in your head. Next, let local awareness move down through your neck and into your chest, and know directly from within your upper body.

4. Become familiar with this direct knowing from within; it neither looks down from your head nor looks back up to your thoughts.

5. Feel the awareness and aliveness together: rest without going to sleep and stay aware without going to thought to know.

6. Notice a feeling of an open heart space from within the center of your chest.

7. Feel as if you have relocated from your head to this open heart space, from which you are now knowing and aware.

8. Notice that you can invite and welcome any thoughts down so that you can remain at home in your heart and still have information from the office of your head come to you as if by Wi-Fi.

9. Be here, receive light with your eyes, and look out from the eyes of open-hearted awareness.

10. Feel how local awareness can move back, through the door of your heart, to the space behind your body.

11. Surrender local awareness behind your body until local awareness mingles with spacious awareness that's already aware.

12. Wait until you are knowing from the timeless, spacious, thought-free awareness.

13. Now notice that this field of awareness-energy is also including your whole body.

14. Notice how local awareness is also moving forward and looking out at the world through your heart space.

15. Be aware from this field of awareness-energy—behind, within and in front. It's simultaneously spacious and pervasive: a continuous field of interconnected awareness-energy.

16. Notice that awareness-energy is both outside and inside at the same time.

17. Without going to thought ask, *What does open-hearted awareness know?*

18. Simply let go and let be. Rest in this new knowing and flowing; see from being.

19. Notice the loving awareness happening effortlessly. ■

GLIMPSE **Cave of the Heart**

This practice is similar to the yogic meditation practice called *nirvikalpa samadhi*, a practice of absorption without any self-referencing, and what Tibetans call the practice of "the mind of black near-attainment." It's also similar to *yoga nidra* (yogic sleep), a practice of deep rest. You may know the yoga nidra practice *shavasana*, commonly done at the end of yoga classes, which has great benefits for resting the entire nervous system on a deep level.

Cave of the Heart is a practice in which you can experience no-self in a way that's more restful than sleep, yet you remain wide awake without content or a small self. Many of the glimpses shift us into a pristine, infinite day-sky view. In the Cave of the Heart practice, the experience of no-self is like the infinite night sky, an experience of black-velvet awareness.

The twentieth-century Hindu sage Ramana Maharshi often recommended two practices. One was the classical self-inquiry "Who Am I?" The second practice he recommended, which is less well known, he referred to as "resting in the cave of the heart on the right side of the chest." He never described in much detail how to do this practice, but I played around with it to see what it felt like. I found that in using local awareness to go within the cave of the heart, it seemed to open up a profound dimension of awareness. Here's a version that makes sense to me and that seems to work for many others. Many of my students say this is one of their favorite practices.

On the left side of your chest is your biological heart. The heart chakra—or energy center—has been described as being in the middle of the chest. On the right side of the chest is the cave of the heart—the safe space of the heart. It's where the physical heart would be if it were on the right side of your chest—but instead, there is a space.

In this mindful glimpse, we unhook local awareness from thought and drop it down to the safe, restful place that is the cave of the heart. As I mentioned, it's a way of resting deeper than sleep, though we are wide awake. When our body rests deeply, the normal tendency is for our mind to fall asleep. Here, when you allow your body and brain to rest deeply, see if there's also an awareness that remains wide awake—a black-velvet purity, like the night sky.

Some people report that a short period of resting in the cave of the heart makes them feel like they've had the equivalent of the best full-night's sleep of their life. Enjoy.

1. Sit comfortably or lie on your back. Close your eyes and take a full breath or two so that you feel alert, alive, and awake.

2. Now allow local awareness to unhook from thought. Let it slowly drift down like a leaf below your neck and find a safe, restful place inside your upper body

on the right side of your chest. This safe space may feel like it has a little light or pinpoints of light, or it may be completely dark, like black velvet.

3. Allow your awareness to rest in this black-velvet silence without falling asleep. Feel each cell drinking in this rest and renewal. Let awake awareness surrender into the cave of the heart and rest as this deep, dazzling darkness, deeper than sleep, yet wide awake. Remain here for ten to fifteen minutes or until you naturally arise or open your eyes. ■

I hope these mindful glimpses have opened you to new forms of awareness and shifts in perception. The more you practice them, the more you will learn to abide as your true Self. Give yourself patience and gentleness, and make sure you bring a sense of curiosity to it and enjoy it! You can use this chapter as a reference anytime in your day-to-day life. You can explore and choose your favorites. Don't forget that you can make your own voice recordings of these mindful glimpses to listen to at your own pacing.

Part III
Abiding

7

The Ultimate Medicine of No-self Self

Many people have longed and strived to know their true Self. One reason we can't find Self, see it, or understand it is because Self is not an "it." Self is not an object or thing that can be seen, heard, touched, smelled, tasted, or known by thought. It isn't an emotion, image, belief, feeling, or even energy. This is why some traditions begin by emphasizing that there is no solid, separate self. By using the term "no-self Self" or just "Self," I am bridging the no-self insight with our vast open-hearted awareness and the conventional, human level of reality. So far in this book, we've mostly been practicing shifting out of thinking mind and exploring different forms of awareness, and now we'll transition to understanding who we are: our identity. We'll do this by shifting out of our small self and into no-self and then uncovering our true Self, which I'll refer to as capital-S Self.

When we discover open-hearted awareness, we realize that our small sense of self is not truly who we are. When we look closely here, we see there is not one small self, but there is not just an absence of self either, as we have many parts of our personality.

Once we have shifted our identity from a small self to experiencing the spaciousness of no-self through awake awareness, we are free as we realize that our small sense of self is not truly who we are. However, as we look back at where our small self was located from awareness-energy, we have the funny experience of realizing that even though there isn't one small self, there are multiple subpersonalities within us. We see our own thoughts and emotions as constellations of consciousness, or subpersonalities, which I will call *parts* of us. In the practice of insight meditation, we break down our small self into even smaller elements of thoughts, feelings, and sensations. However, while engaging in daily life, these thoughts, feelings, and sensations come together and manifest as parts, so it is helpful to learn how to address this level. This is the process we'll be covering in this chapter.

I've asked clients to become aware of an anxious part and then a less anxious part of themselves. When asked who is aware of those two parts, they often respond, "Me." I have then asked, "Where are you aware from?" They have responded, "All around," or "Within my heart," or "From everywhere." I was amazed at how even people who had diagnosed mental illnesses and complex trauma benefitted from directly accessing Self. I started to adapt and refine this process of realizing Self and brought the two disciplines of meditation and psychology together in my psychotherapy practice and teaching. I have found that distinguishing small self from Self is accessible and relatable for clients and students when it comes to understanding how awakening, psychological growth, and healing overlap.

The Experience of Self

The Self has been the most valued human dimension in most cultures and contemplative traditions throughout history. Our interconnected Self has been called being, true nature, nature of mind, sacred heart, unity consciousness, no-self Self, unchanging essence, open-hearted awareness, and optimal mind. Self has often been associated with religious traditions and considered spiritual. However, Self can simply be understood as the subtlest essential dimension of the human consciousness we all share, regardless of belief.

Self is you, but not the "you" that you often think you are. Self is the "I am" without I am "this" or I am "that." Self is not the thinker. Self is not your personality, not your ego or observing ego, not a hypnotic or altered state, not an image or your imagination, not an archetype or a separate soul, not a guide or inner voice, not solely an energy, not an entity or the human person that you are today. Self is neither meditator nor detached mindful witness. Self is aware of all these experiences, states, and parts; Self is inherent within them and includes them.

Self is not created, developed, or conditioned. Self is. Everyone is already Self. Self is within us, around us, and is us: it is who we truly are. Self is closer than our breath, and Self, like breath, happens automatically, spontaneously, without any effort. Self feels "centered" but not centered in our head or a distinct part. Many people say it feels like a "centerless center," which is both embodied and free. Self is essentially the same within each of us, and each person is a unique expression of Self.

Self is inherent within us even when the "clouds" of our beliefs, emotions, feelings, perceptions, and identifications obscure it. Self loves and can safeguard all parts. Self is also within all parts. Self can know parts just as parts can learn to know Self.

Self is our natural context, which is always present, but can become hidden when blended with our parts. Discovering the fullness of Self is described by many people as "returning home." Losing a sense of Self is often the feeling of being contracted into a point of view, blended with a part that sits in the seat of "I," so the part believes it is "me."

Although Self is who we have always been and includes the loving presence we have been looking for, parts may initially protect against feeling Self because it is so boundless. But parts long for Self, and they all are ultimately happy to unburden and have Self lead. For example, people who identify with feeling inadequate and experience shame may truly believe that there is something wrong with them. There is a way to step outside of the part that has that fixed belief, view it from the outside, and interact with it. Accessing Self, and welcoming all parts, has been called "the ultimate medicine" because it relieves the root of suffering, which is, paradoxically, caused by not experiencing or living from the Self that we are.

Self is innate and whole and has different dimensions. Self appears as different expressions of itself—like water when it is ice, liquid, steam, or invisible humidity. All dimensions of Self are always here; however, when we are blended with a part, we are neither aware of Self nor aware from Self. When this happens, we are only aware of our part from our part, and we think that the part is all there is. Our world then becomes much smaller. We can even subscribe to our part's worldview that we are "not good enough" and subtly give up in one area of life.

This brings us back to how Self can be distinguished from a part through the process of unblending. *Unblending* is a process of disidentifying with parts and identifying with Self, our magnificent essence. When we are blended, not only do we believe we are that dominant part, but that part believes it is us. We'll play with unblending in the mindful glimpse at the end of this chapter, but first consider how unblending begins: by helping parts trust that it is safe for them to relax. We can unblend by asking the part for more space between Self and that part. As we do this, it is important to show respect to the blended parts; otherwise, they will double down in strength, feeling unseen, and try even harder to receive acknowledgment. For example, if we judge our judging part, it will get stronger and more protective. It seems illogical to welcome and give love to angry or mean parts of us, but this is what seems to be the secret to liberating us.

We will know we've shifted from parts to Self when our perspective goes from feeling located in a contracted place, looking out from a point of view inside the body (usually from behind the eyes), to viewing from open-hearted awareness, which is simultaneously within, boundless, and interconnected.

Self can sometimes be distinguished by asking, *Am I aware from my head or from my heart?* or *In this Self-to-part relationship, how open is my heart toward that part?* The heart-knowing from Self is not just from what you might think of as your physical heart, heart chakra, or emotional heart, but rather from your natural, wise heart-mind. This always already open-hearted awareness is waiting patiently to be uncovered and lived from.

Self is what is here when everything else falls away. Self doesn't try to exist. Self is beyond the qualities, states, beliefs, emotions, expressions, or identities that we cycle through. Self is the constant. For many people, Self first reveals itself in silence, when the noise falls away. Self is extraordinarily simple. Self has no agenda, no striving, no grasping, no aversion. It needs nothing because it is and has everything. Self is the foundation before the identity we wear, like the nakedness before the clothing that we put on. We often think the clothing is "me," but Self is the naked awareness under this "me."

When we talk about "ego personality self," we're talking about the clothing or each of the articles of clothing, because there are often many component parts! As we come to experience life increasingly from our interconnected Self, we notice the parts of us that come and go. We can observe, get to know, and care for these parts.

More than the Sum of the Parts

When I returned from my fellowship in Sri Lanka, India, and Nepal, I began practicing a form of mindfulness-based psychotherapy that I called Effortless Mindfulness Based Therapy (EMBT). This was a unique mindfulness approach that was not based in cognitive therapy but instead in body and subpersonality psychotherapies, such as Jungian, Gestalt, and Psychosynthesis. In recent years, I've been collaborating with Richard Schwartz, the founding developer of the Internal Family Systems (IFS) model of psychotherapy. We have had long talks and discovered we were each using similar systems of Self and parts. He had come up with a simple and clear way of accessing and defining parts, and I had focused on developing a simple and clear way of accessing and defining Self. As a result, I have adopted his elegant and thorough map of parts when I work with clients. What we teach complements each other, and we have taught a number of workshops and retreats together.

The IFS model describes the nature of the human psyche as organizing into subpersonalities, or parts, that all come together within the Self. The goal of this therapy is not to judge, minimize, or get rid of these parts, but instead to notice and lovingly embrace all of our parts from our interconnected Self, which is also within all parts.

Both models of psychotherapy—EMBT and IFS—present paths toward the relief of suffering and becoming more whole and authentic. The centerpiece of each is our "capital-S" Self because only a limited level of psychological healing and growth can happen without realizing Self. What's more, this approach is empowering because it shows us that it is our own true Self—rather than another person or external teachings—that actively provides the deepest and most complete healing.

Schwartz clearly explains how what we often call the ego personality, the psyche, or the small self is a composition of parts or subpersonalities that take on certain roles and interact with each other. For example, we may experience a part of ourselves that feels anger and then another part of ourselves that feels shame about the anger and then another part of ourselves that tries to manage what we should do about that anger and shame. In this way, our thoughts and beliefs can be experienced as little personalities within us that behave according to their own worldview. It's the natural state of the mind to be multiple. Events from childhood burden parts, force them into extreme roles, and make them feel disconnected from Self.

For example, many of us have had early shame-based thoughts that are about trying to understand who we are, such as, "I'm not good enough," or "I'm unlovable." These are the mistaken views that are the burdens carried by our parts. When these burdened parts take over, our view of life is limited by their perspective. As we get to know our parts, even the most difficult ones, we can discover the insight of IFS therapy that all parts are looking for love, and there are no bad parts.

I've combined Schwartz's insights with my method of experiential ways of accessing Self—the whole of who we truly are beyond any part—as a technique for embodying and living an awakened life. I particularly find this the most effective way of healing our shadows—those unconscious, repressed, or denied parts. This approach helps to create a positive feedback loop for awakening: First, our practice of effortless mindfulness helps us access our greater context of true Self, through which we can work with our parts. In turn, doing our parts work heals and unburdens us on a psychological level so that we can more easily uncover and maintain the wholeness, coherence, and peace of our true Self that can allow for sustained awakening. Learning effortless mindfulness as a foundation can change what would have been a "dark night of the soul" into more of a detox or thawing-out process, with more growing pains than unconscious suffering. The way of effortless mindfulness gives access to the resource of Self, which can bear what seemed to be unbearable.

Knowing and Liberating Parts

The clouds that obscure our already awake loving nature often take the form of hurt parts of us that are all trying to find safety and love. Our parts fit into distinct categories, each with different reasons for being. In the IFS model, our parts are categorized as:

- Managers (These protector parts try to protect through different daily roles.)

- Exiles (These are the hurt parts, which are often repressed, usually storing trauma.)

- Firefighters (These are the parts that emerge in crisis and act strongly when exiles are upset.)

We experience our subpersonalities when we say things like, "One part of me is angry at my partner, but another part understands why they said that." Or we might discover in psychotherapy how a young part of us was burdened. For example, someone dealing with low self-esteem might remember something like this: "When I was a child, my mother took a long time to come and feed me. I felt the pain of hunger and grew terrified that I had been abandoned. On some level, I started to believe that there must be something wrong with me: I must be worthless or unlovable." The burdens of exiles, managers, and firefighters emerge organically for everyone, regardless of the type or style of parenting we experienced. IFS and EMBT are ways of doing shadow work with parts that are hidden, denied, or repressed, such as exiles and firefighters, to effectively bring such unconscious parts into the conscious light of healing.

These patterns create neuronal networks in the brain that are like scenes from a movie that keep replaying. When these networks are activated and reactivated in the brain, nervous system, and body through a triggering event, they overtake us with primal force. This can cause us to regress, making us think or even behave as if we're the age when the trauma originally occurred. It can feel like we are that hurt child looking through our adult eyes. We may feel overtaken by a damaged worldview or by strong feelings and motivations, such as protective, defensive rage.

A triggering event is an event in the present that is similar to a traumatic event in the past that was too overwhelming. Even though the experiences may have been real when they happened, they are not happening in the present. Parts are not "you" now, but when triggered, they feel and act like they are you. If they are treated like they are only thoughts or feelings arising, they may seem to go away temporarily, but they return. Even though it seems counterintuitive, talking to these parts of us as if they were the little beings they think they are is the radical shift I offer in this healing paradigm. When parts can be loved and healed back to their innocent childlike nature, they are liberated by your whole Self. When the inner child is listened to, the misunderstandings unburdened, and its emotions felt by Self, parts frozen in time or stuck in an emotional loop can become integrated elements of a complete, healthy human.

Some of the initial work that needs to take place for this synthesis to occur can be done prior to initial awakening through psychotherapy and other personal-growth techniques. However, it is only possible to do this work of waking up and growing up fully from Self, which is why practicing effortless mindfulness is key. It provides the capacity to access our Self. When we're able to shift our identity in this way, we have more capacity and deeper love to care for our parts.

Much of this healing can be done in our daily lives, but there is also great benefit to having someone, such as a therapist or experienced meditation teacher, guide and support you through the introduction of parts to Self. This process leads to the moment when we realize that parts exist, why they arose, and that they are not ultimately the true Self. It is then that we can distinguish our true Self from the parts. Often, the first step is experiencing our parts from our mindful witness, which is a Self-like part. A Self-like part is a manager, a *spiritual ego* that has many of the qualities of Self but still has the agenda of a part. Gradually, we can learn to access Self to embrace our parts with love and to integrate toward deep wholeness. Eventually, we can treat other people's parts with the same understanding we've given our own, so when we encounter someone acting from a hurt or manager part, we realize what's occurring and find a way to respond with empathy rather than react with fear-based judgment.

It's important to notice how we might be in the habit of trying to find solutions for our troubles by using tactics of our small mind and small self. Often, when we view our emotions from our small self, we view some emotions as "good" and some as "bad" and then try to transform destructive emotions into constructive emotions. In doing so, we may reinforce the manager part or small self that is trying to heal our emotions. However, no small self, managing part, or ego identity can live a fully intimate, emotional life. This attempt will lead to some form of neurosis, anxiety, depression, or addiction. Instead, we can learn to access our original Self, which has the natural capacity to feel, create, and love.

Some parts react to this by trying to help, by becoming smart workaholics, angry managers, or protectors of the exiled inner children. For example, if an inner child part feels needy, an angry protector part, who believes that neediness will lead to rejection from others, may jump in, and in a faulty attempt at protecting may self-blame, telling the child part to "stop crying and get a grip!" The unique beauty of the IFS approach is that we don't try to fight our protector parts, get rid of them, replace them, or even transform these "negative" managers or protectors into positive feelings. Instead, like the exiled child parts, these manager and firefighter parts need love to be unburdened and release the role they feel they have to play. This is done when our true Self understands, respects, and appreciates the "difficult" parts and thanks them for trying to help as they deemed best.

I've learned from my own experiences and from my psychotherapy clients that it is best to meet each part in the way it appears. So rather than just witnessing thoughts, feelings, stories, and beliefs, the most healing approach seems to be listening to and unburdening these parts by interacting with them with love. The primary way is to have a therapist lead you through this process to go inward and feel each part within your body and locate their shape, size, color, and emotional tone. Then honor and thank the part, and ask the part if it would give you some space. Then, from the space, begin to feel a sense of true Self, which feels at first like open space. This allows for some detachment as well as some foundation of Self in awake awareness rather than another thought-based part. Then our Self is asked directly, "How do You feel toward that part?" When we are in Self, we feel a connection, which is called Self-energy, which feels compassion toward the parts.

Psychological Underpass

All our parts—whether hurt or protective, angry or defensive—work toward making everything feel okay. It is important not to minimize, reject, or try to get rid of our strong emotional parts. For example, if we try to meditate negative feelings away, we end up in a "spiritual bypass"—only focusing on the transcendent dimension, experiencing ourselves as awake awareness but numb and distant from the parts of us that are still uninte-grated and not meeting them the way they need to be met.

When identity remains in "I think, therefore I am," and we try to deal with our parts by intellectualizing or rationalizing them away, I call this a "cognitive overpass." We can't transcend our hurt exiles, our protective parts, our emotional trauma, or our full relational human-ity. If we have a psychology that doesn't have this larger dimension of Self, we can end up in what I call a *psychological underpass*—reducing our primary identity and tools of healing to biology, ego managers, emotions, cognition, and personality, trying to tend to our parts from a helpful manager part that can be skilled but is not our true Self. This is why it is so important to practice effortless mindfulness: so that we can get to know and act from our true Self.

We can go deeper into exploring our ways of attempting to help from the small self. Returning to the spiritual bypass, consider that we might alternatively find ourselves going to a no-self detached witness that is ignoring some parts, which doesn't resolve anything in the long term. For example, if you feel jealous or angry, and you treat those feelings as destructive emotions and then use deliberate mindfulness to see them in a neutral way or try to transform them with a managing part or positive antidotes of lovingkindness, they may diminish or seem to go away, but the jealous or angry part that was not wanted is still somewhere within your consciousness feeling unwanted and dismissed. This jealous or angry part takes its burdens and feelings and goes back into the shadows until it is triggered again.

The cognitive overpass is trickier. Here, our rational manager or mindful witness will show up within us to acknowledge that we are caught in some kind of suffering. The rational manager and mindful witness are more developed parts, but they are still just parts, so we remain limited in the parts-based small-self system.

When you confuse your true identity with a part of you that is caught in ignorance or attachment—a psychological underpass—it is not just that you believe you are an angry part; more importantly, the angry part believes it is you and becomes you and acts and reacts like it is you. While being identified as the part, we address the emotion, trying to be less angry, more accepting, or more vulnerable. We can only get so far in healing without discovering the Self that has natural vulnerability and courage.

The spiritual bypass, cognitive overpass, and psychological underpass are attempts to heal parts from other parts! This doesn't work. We can't experience full integration because our parts do not have the capacity of healing love. Only our true Self is bigger than and beyond all of our conditioning. So the important thing is to find the Self that has the capacity to bear what seemed to be unbearable, the Self that can be with these parts and love them.

Sometimes, though, it's hard to tell if we're meeting parts from a Self-like part, especially when we make a cognitive overpass when we are not used to experiencing ourselves outside of the small mind. It is common to want to escape the small mind—and everything else—so badly that we end up in the spiritual bypass! The key is to be gentle with ourselves and with all of our parts, including the parts of us that are worried if we're doing this work incorrectly or judging ourselves for "not getting it."

When you check to see where Self is, who is looking? Only the interconnected Self all around and within all parts can know itself. Self is not a state that appears to you. This is because Self is you! As a way of unblending your Self from Self-like parts, you can ask, *Is this part aware of me?* which will shift you to locate your Self beyond the part, creating an amazing opportunity to know Self directly from the Self.

The Three Facets of Self

Just as it is possible to distinguish and know our parts as managers, exiles, and firefighters, we can learn to know three aspects of Self. Richard Schwartz divides Self into "Self-energy" and "Self-leadership," to which I've added "Self-essence." These can be described briefly as follows:

- *Self-essence* is the way we experience Self with awake awareness—pure Self, the authentic fundamental nature of who we are: invisible, intelligent awake awareness.

- *Self-energy* is our Self knowing parts and other people and experiencing from awareness-energy through being relational and connected.

- *Self-leadership* is grounded in Self-essence and Self-energy becoming full embodiment of open-hearted awareness, where we can live our daily life from.

Notice that each aspect of Self has a quality we have covered through the lens of awareness. Now we're looking at how we can experience our felt sense of identity, who we are, in congruence with these types of awareness.

FACET ONE   SELF-ESSENCE

As we've explored in these pages, awake awareness is intelligence prior to thought that is invisible yet palpable. Self-essence is not found as either inside versus outside but is both spacious and pervasive, transcendent and immanent—everywhere, nowhere in particular, and very much here. Because it is wordless, and not a thing or an object, we might overlook it. Self-essence—invisible intelligent awareness—is our boundless ground.

In my process of understanding and teaching Self-essence, I've come up with eleven **I**s to illustrate it:

Invisible	Intelligent	Innate
Is	Indestructible	Infinite
Immediate	Illumined	Inherent
Inspired	Ineffable	

Self-essence does not change or grow, it just is. Self-essence cannot be hurt or destroyed. Self-essence is often difficult to see because we see from Self-essence. From Self-essence there is seeing the whole without the feeling of a particular location of a seer. Self-essence is the foundation of all expressions of Self, although its subtlety is often not felt directly because it is so close, so invisible, and is not a state.

Self-essence is not known as an object but knows itself first as awake awareness. It is unconditioned and is inherent within our conditioning and precedes energy: it is that from which energy arises. We can learn to let parts know that they are safe to give us more space or to step back to discover Self-essence. Self-essence is the transcendent clear light of awareness.

FACET TWO   SELF-ENERGY

Self-essence arises or comes into existence as energy. It is like the quantum field: Self-essence is an invisible source, prior to energy. In turn, Self-energy is both wave—flowing boundless dynamism with relational qualities—and particle—active, compassionate, embodied, and full of vitality. The waves and particles are made of the invisible potential of the quantum field of Self-essence.

Self-energy is connected through the type of awake awareness we know as awareness-energy. It is how we feel the sense of interconnected relationship from Self to parts within us and with other people and all things around us. It is from Self-essence that Self-energy's natural qualities arise as creative energetic expressions. Self-energy is the healing light of liberation, as there is the capacity for movement, expression, and transformation.

The qualities of Self-energy, or eight **C**s,[1] created by Schwartz are:

Calm	Curiosity	Compassion
Confidence	Courage	Clarity
Connectedness	Creativity	

FACET THREE   SELF-LEADERSHIP

Self is grounded in Self-essence, interconnected and related through Self-energy, and acts from Self-leadership. Self-leadership is the ability to create and relate from open-hearted awareness and heart-mind. With Self-leadership, we unblend and shift the location of our identity from parts to Self. In Self-leadership, we can feel the spacious awareness of Self-essence and Self-energy's dynamic aliveness, full embodiment, and the compassionate relationship to all parts and people. From Self-leadership, you can make choices while being free of the agendas of parts. Being in Self-leadership does not get rid of parts or reduce parts to a smoothie, but, as Dan Siegel says, it is more like a colorful fruit salad of parts.[2]

Schwartz's nine **P**s of Self-leadership[3] are:

Patience	Persistence	Perspective
Presence	Pure Perception	Peace
Precision	Purpose	Playfulness

In Self-leadership, we speak for parts rather than from parts. Self knows that all is well while also having the motivation to actively be part of the solutions in the world. Self-leadership operates from our compassionate, wise heart-mind connected to Self-essence, as if using Wi-Fi to bring personal information and memory files down from the office of our head to our new home in our heart-mind. Self-leadership feels grounded in Self-essence, feels itself within our body, and feels the parts with Self-energy as it looks out from the eyes of the heart to people and to the world with new motivation and vision for action. Self-leadership is simultaneously aware of all the dimensions of Self, our parts, and other people and the world. Self-leadership has the light of compassionate wisdom in action.

Your Self-Driving Vehicle

What I've done above is look at awake awareness, awareness-energy, and open-hearted awareness through the lens of Self. This is who we are and how we are being when we are experiencing different levels of awareness. Note that language becomes tricky here: Self and awake awareness are two views of the same thing. We *are* that awake awareness, and we call it by the name of whatever "Self" term correlates with it. The difference is in the nuance: when we talk about awake awareness, we talk about perception, how we are perceiving; when we talk about Self, we talk about identity and who we perceive ourselves to be.

It is important to note that overly emphasizing one dimension of Self without staying connected to all dimensions of Self can lead to an imbalance—bypassing, underpassing, or overpassing. If we are overly focused on Self-essence, we can become spaced out, transcendent, and impersonally detached. Imbalanced Self-energy can lead to taking on other people's emotional energy or continually moving parts around on the chessboard of the psyche. It can also lead to being a "bliss ninny," "hippy-happy," or an unmotivated couch potato.

Being too imbalanced in trying to be in Self-leadership from a part can lead to becoming an outwardly focused helper or an activist who burns out by feeling disconnected and not resourcing with the Source of Self. Notice, though, that Self-leadership, as open-hearted aware-ness, is indeed how I'm defining our interconnected whole, true Self. So when I point out this imbalance related to Self-leadership, it is not that Self-leadership itself is imbalanced, but instead, what will tie us in knots is an attempt to be in Self-leadership when we are in a part that is thinking that it is true Self when it is not. What's necessary is acquiring the discernment to tell the difference—as sometimes we can have blind spots! This is when it is helpful to be reflected by friends, a healing practitioner, or even paying attention to cause and effect from our actions and choices.

It is from the heart-mind, the all-embracing, compassionate, open-hearted awareness of Self-leadership, that we are able to meet and embrace our parts. When we do, we recognize them and bring them back to Self so that we can have integration and wholeness. A good way to do this is with some mindful glimpses.

GLIMPSE **Know Your Self**

Recognizing Self leads us to a new kind of Self-compassion practice. In the usual self-compassion practices, who is compassionate to whom? What self is compassionate to what self? This usually means that a part is trying to have compassion for another part. In the following approach, we realize that who we are is not a small self but many parts. Then, rather than a part having compassion for different parts of "yourself," there is a discovery of Self, which has natural compassion for the whole. This mindful glimpse can also be done with another person.

1. Can you feel an emotional or energetic pattern you're aware of in or around your body? What is the shape, size, location, and feeling of this part?

2. Can you thank this part and ask it to unblend and open some space?

3. From this space, rest as the awareness that is aware. How do you feel toward this part, not from your head but from your heart? Is this part aware that you are here with it? Is this part aware of your feelings toward it?

4. Is there anything this part wants to let you know?

5. When this part turns to be aware of You, what does it experience as the size, location, and feeling of You?

6. How does it feel to be aware from your heart toward this pattern within your body?

7. How is it being open-hearted Self with your body and these parts? ■

Accessing Our True Self

Now that we've reviewed three types of Self that correlate with the three types of awareness we've covered previously, we can notice and practice how infinite, dynamic, loving, and capable of meeting life our true Self is in all of its aspects. We can realize that we are this infinite, loving Self, and whenever we feel disconnected and contracted, we're probably in a part of us—a part that somehow got cut off from the whole and has forgotten "home." When we're fully identified with that part, thinking that that is "me," we end up living life through its lens and act through its beliefs and agendas, which might create havoc! Instead, when we take a step back to unblend from whatever part we are blended with, we can remember how to unhook awareness to return to our Self-essence. Then, from Self-energy, we can see the part we were blended with and begin to listen to its story. Then, from Self-leadership, we can finally embrace our parts and welcome them back home to our Self. Each time we get to know the exiled parts in this way, we become increasingly aware of our wholeness. From here, we're ready to move on to sustained awakening—training to remain awake from Self-leadership.

8

How to Remain Awake

The most fundamental aspect of awakening is the shift in our understanding of who we are. Our culture, upbringing, and mind have all created a sense of "me" that is based on a thinking self: "I think, therefore I am." Even when experiencing awake awareness, awareness-energy, or open-hearted awareness, we have missed the point if we think that these experiences are "cool meditation states" and then return to our regular lives. These types of awareness are not states of mind; these are dimensions of our interconnected, whole Self. Shifting into Self is not just an exercise of imagination or a psychological practice that our thinking parts do when we are in crisis or feel a need to care for our hurt child parts. Experiencing life through the eyes of our true Self is our natural human potential.

We take the first step on the path to awakening when we realize that we are a different Self than we originally understood. When we taste this shift in identity, it is an "aha!" moment. We feel like we have seen behind the veil of separation and understood something so crucial that we never forget it. We realize that we are so much more capable of love and more whole than we ever imagined.

This initial shift can often be experienced as deep relief, letting go, or a sense of homecoming. From our shift of Self, we are able to see how we are compassionate creators in the world, how we are lovable no matter what, and how our problems are held within something much larger. We are happier and more fulfilled than we could have imagined because there is no conditionality to our well-being; we intimately feel how we are innately perfect and well. Once we directly experience this reality, even if just for a moment, we may feel changed at our core (although we have not changed into something new but rather come into our true Self that has been there the whole time).

Once we experience a shift into Self, something funny happens: often, even if we think our realization will last forever, eventually we find ourselves back in a more contracted, habitual experience of small self. While we may have thought that living from our awareness of our true Self would easily continue, we come to realize that we need to go through an unfolding process for our awakening to abide as Self-leadership. By "abide," I mean a background-to-foreground shift, where open-hearted awareness remains primary and becomes where we are viewing and living from. Abiding is a dynamic moment-to-moment unfolding within the ground of awake awareness that does not come and go.

From the ultimate level of reality, we could say there is no process of abiding, no journey, and no path. The essential awake awareness is always present and does not change or develop. Awake awareness is already abiding, even when our human experiences are changing and passing away. The small self does not awaken, and the true Self is not a stable entity or person. Awakening is simply a shift of view to look at the interconnected whole from open-hearted awareness. We have explored how there is no-self, and yet this does not lead to us being robots or puppets of awake awareness. There is a play of yin/yang, Shakti/Shiva, divine/human, transcendent/immanent, which is a dance of formless awake awareness and our human form.

I have met people who have had an initial waking up from small self who get stuck in this first stage in the unfolding of full awakening. This is because initial waking up is not enough, and there is no one so evolved that they do not have to go through an unfolding process to live from an embodied open-hearted awareness. As we awaken, we do not become perfect by any means, but we do have a wholly different way of knowing, being, and experiencing life than we did when we were identified with a smaller ego-self. We can delve even deeper by examining what goes on during this stage of awakening into Self-leadership.

Why It Is Hard to Remain in Self-Leadership

The first hint about why it is hard to remain in Self-leadership is that the "you" that wants to remain awake is not you! The entire abiding experience will feel paradoxical to the thinking manager "you," which will likely think that nothing on this path of awakening makes any sense! Indeed, the reason many people haven't yet awakened is because the small self is being run by their survival operating system and the expectations of our culture.

Here is where a transitionally helpful spiritual ego, meditator, manager, or Self-like part can be a trap if not recognized. This is where a wise teacher, like a good car mechanic, who has been through the transitions from small self to Self-leadership can give pointers for maintenance of your Self-driving vehicle and a tune-up to get you back on the road.

At first, we may think that Self is a part of us or a state, such as silence or stillness, but in order for Self to remain primary—the place we view from rather than what we view—Self must get to know itself. We must avoid being pulled into the mind by the old egoic structure and its defenses, which, for their own survival, are wanting to convince you that Self is just a "meditation state" so that they can remain in the driver's seat—a Self-like part playing the role of Self.

How do we get to know Self? First, we learn how to let go of the small self that is currently leading. We first need to get it out of the driver's seat so greater Self can sit in it (even though it has been waiting in the background the whole time). The key in this effortless mindfulness approach is to shift immediately into the new operating system of awake awareness rather than just deconstructing the small self. Awakening and stabilizing our awakening is as much a process of unlearning as learning. It is going to take effortless mindfulness to change the old habit of remaining in our small self and to learn to let go into open-hearted awareness, which sustains itself naturally.

One student expressed this stage of moving from effort to effortlessness by saying, "Not knowing has been such a gift because it means that I can give up all the trying. I can give up wanting things to be a certain way, and I can just let go. I can't express how free I feel in letting go of that striving. It is then that I notice a new knowing that is alert, safe, and wise. I don't have to go back to my thinking mind to try to confirm anything, and there is so much peace and freedom in that."

This transition into "don't know mind" can feel like the moment we released our parent's hand when we were a kid on the first day of kindergarten. But here, as we move toward the unknown, toward the greater Self, we are letting go of the ego identity's hand. We must learn to bear the arising of unpleasant messages from our ego managers that are yelling "Danger!" from the repressed contents of our psyche and from our protective parts and inner children calling out to be seen and processed. The danger signal at this stage is like a car alarm going off with no threat to the vehicle. Can we sit in the fire of these transitional moments?

The key experience of this stage is a shift through the unknown into the new knowing of awake awareness. We can think about it like swinging on a rope that's hanging from a tree branch that reaches from the shore out over a lake. Letting go of the rope to jump into the water can be frightening because we relinquish control of our grip on safety. The water isn't like the land we left behind, but when we are in it, we'll find that it is a place that brings joy, refreshment, and a new kind of support. This is how it feels to transition from small separate self to interconnected whole Self.

We transition through the gap of "not knowing" for what can be a short or long period of time in our lives when we don't have an understanding of who we really are, what we're doing, or what we're here for. This natural part of the journey can feel scary, but we don't have to get stuck here as we have learned early on to resource with the new operating system of awake awareness.

The Dos and Don'ts of Awakening

A main reason we experience so much unknown is that we are changing drivers in the vehicle that is our sense of self. In the past, we had a competent manager part that was on duty sitting in the driver's seat of our sense of self, vigilant about our experience, managing our choices, and analyzing things. Moving into living from Self requires removing this manager from the driver's seat so that Self can sit there. Self is not a new manager, but it does need to acknowledge and connect to the managers and functional parts of our body and mind.

The small self's strongest survival programming is a series of four "don'ts" and six "shoulds." Here are the four "don'ts" of the small self and the solutions from the interconnected Self:

1. *Don't go out of your mind.* To find your ground of Self, you need to go against your ego's strongest rules of survival. When you do, you end up realizing that it is sane for local awareness to go out of your small mind to discover the source of mind—awake awareness.

2. *Don't become nobody.* As you follow your intention of living as your true Self and let go into the unknown, you will go through a sense of becoming "nobody." Don't worry. This is normal. In this phase, you're not becoming a blank slate or a robot; you are simply not feeling like the somebody you thought you were. As you move through the gap of "nobody" into awake awareness, you'll increasingly start to feel the ground of your Self.

3. *Don't lose control.* The old identity has to lose control and release, let go, or surrender for a moment in order for the new ground of Self to emerge. This can feel disorienting since we've been deeply conditioned to control everything and to desire predictability. But it is a normal and liberating phase of awakening to experience disorientation before reorientation.

4. *Don't stop thinking.* When you stop relying on thought-based knowing, you don't become dumb or ignorant. Instead, you move beyond the dualistic mind's limited way of knowing to a new kind of wisdom that is naturally available.

Here are the six "shoulds" of the small self and the solutions from the interconnected Self:

1. *I should be the small self to know.* How can I know if I don't think? The small self comes in with doubt and fear to say, "You need to go to thought and know conceptually." Instead, there is a new, nonconceptual *not-knowing that knows,* a heart-knowing that is prior to thought. Only when we stop trying to understand things through our dualistic thoughts will we start to receive a direct knowing that can come through a deeper connection to the space and silence of awake awareness.

2. *I should be the small self to be safe.* Who will keep me safe if I don't construct plans and protect myself with vigilance? We are drawn back to the parts-based identity to be safe. Instead, the ground of Self provides a way to be safe without constantly scanning for danger. A new sense of safety emerges as we feel Self beyond the stories of our lives, which is safer than we feel through the ego managers. As for day-to-day safety issues, our intuition shows us the way, and our thinking mind is still available for problem solving when we need it.

   Another safety concern might come up in the mind's eye when we surrender into the gap of no-self on our way to the greater freedom of Self. The deeper level of the small self program is to avoid its own death, so the transition through egolessness or no-self feels like who we are is threatened with nonexistence. The best thing to do here is to know that this experience of no-self as we release from the small self is normal, as is the fear, and they will both naturally pass as we emerge into something greater.

3. *I should be the small self to avoid pain.* We feel like we should return to the parts-based identity to avoid emotional and physical pain. Ironically, it is when we try to

avoid pain that it turns into suffering. Our thinking mind often tries to rationalize away difficult emotions, physical sensations, or painful life events. Our small self does not have the capacity to live a fully intimate, emotional human life because when living from the small self, we can often be avoidant of experience. From Self-leadership, we can lovingly approach pain rather than fearfully avoid it. We can find an acceptance of the normal unpleasant experiences in life and release the suffering that we have about our pain. We operate from an awareness that is able to be with unpleasant feelings without pushing them away and is able to be with pleasant feelings without clinging to them. Our inner intelligence can also distinguish between real danger signals, false alarms, and growing pains.

4. *I should be the small self to function.* We may feel that we should return to the parts-based identity to take actions and do things in the world. Indeed, the small mind and ego functioning are superb at certain tasks, such as problem solving, planning, and other types of organizing. It is important to note that in growing from small self to greater Self, we are not abandoning the small mind; we are no longer pretending that the small mind is what "I" am. Instead, "I" can use the thinking mind as a tool, among other tools to choose from. As we shift from parts-based identity to Self, there is a rewiring that allows us to remain at home in heart-knowing and access information without going back to create a "doer," or small self. From here, we can respond rather than react.

5. *I should be separate in order to have loving relationships with others.* Individuation is indeed important as a developmental stage for human beings—to learn a sense of autonomy, to know boundaries, to be able to feel and ask for our needs. Moving from small self to interconnected Self does not

mean dissipating our boundaries, being a codependent personality that just gives in to everyone else's needs, or being too vulnerable to function in relationship. We keep the skills we have learned in our individuation process. We are simply including and transcending individual body-mind as the location of identity. We can keep our individuation as a location point in time and space while we simultaneously operate as and from something much bigger.

Another way we can get caught in the illusion of needing to be separate is if we believe that we are lovable specifically due to our small self. We feel like we should focus on our personality, our looks, and the way we act to be loved. In other words, in this case, we are still seeing love as conditional—conditional upon who we make ourselves to be. Instead, from Self, we experience that love is who we already are. We are love, and we are lovable unconditionally.

6. *I should try to improve the small self to become awake.* This one is the trickiest obstacle because it is difficult to notice when it is happening. This is when the small self "grows up" as much as it can and thinks that it is true Self. Because the small self thinks it should become more developed and smarter, it is unwilling to let go in order to grow. When students say, "I can't do it," they are actually right. That "I" can't do it!

The small self desperately screams, "Do not leave me! If I am not in charge, I will die!" But this is not what will happen. While doing the job of the ego function, the ego managers have mistakenly taken on the role of identity. In awakening, they semi-retire from working the job of identity and return to their natural job of ego function.

In terms of waking up and growing up, it is important to note that when the ego strengths, which were vital for our previous stage of development, form into ego identity, this acts as the main obstacle to the next stage of development and into true Self.

Living from Self-Leadership

We have believed ourselves to be the parts-based ego identity for so long that letting go to grow beyond it can feel like death. What is dying is the identity role that the manager parts have been playing; what is dying is the lens through which you viewed Self and reality. However, this dying allows for a transition into what can also feel like rebirth. This kind of dying is like a seed that has to be buried underground to sprout through the soil and grow to its bigger nature as a tree. It requires a complete letting go—a release or surrender.

This kind of surrender does not happen if we fight, push, resist, or exert too much effort. While the small self does go through a kind of death, it doesn't die if we try to kill it. Nor can it be fought, or even improved, into the interconnected Self. It is important to respect that our ego managers are not our enemies; they have developed to protect us, and they have protected us when we needed them. They deserve honor, not destruction.

What happens if we fight them, deny them, or try to shove them away? Most people who have tried to get rid of their egos have reported that the battle ends up strengthening the ego defenses or creates a Self-like spiritual ego manager. When this happens, our personality can become similar to that of a religious fundamentalist who is convinced of their beliefs but judges everyone else. The ego manager who now takes the role as spiritual know-it-all will still be holding a false sense of control and "knowledge" of how things are, without truly submitting to the don't-know mind or relinquishing the personal will in order for the natural flow of open-hearted awareness to guide our actions.

These managers have not yet allowed for humility to leave space for the awakened Self to be fully open to the unknown. The "spiritual manager" can also do a great job at keeping certain tendencies—like overcontrol or intellectualization—out of our awareness, blinding us to areas of growth we need to integrate. While reading about these spiritual traps and detours, it is helpful to remember that there are gradations of these tendencies rather than "I have that" or "I don't have that anymore." Most of us undergo all of these processes to a certain extent. They are deeply wired in us!

Transitioning out of our conditioned ways is an unfolding. Self rarely remains at the seat of our conscious awareness after the initial glimpse. The ego managers have established deep habits that prioritize safety and survival according to their programming, and the perceived need for safety continues to reconstitute ego defenses that obscure awake awareness. But these innocent habits of our old conditioning will gradually subside as a new connection to the ground of Self and heart-knowing stabilizes.

Because Self naturally has qualities of acceptance, patience, compassion, warmth, and equanimity, we begin to have a baseline of these qualities at all times in a way that we didn't have before, and over time, that baseline grows stronger. For example, a student told me, "Nowadays, I've noticed that no matter what is happening in my work or relationships, I feel good even when I don't feel good." Remarkably, we can experience an essential happiness regardless of what's going on in our daily lives. We feel an underlying well-being because Self is not dependent on conditions or on the ongoing difficulties and delights of daily life.

Peer Inquiries

Awakening is not solely an individual journey; we all affect each other, making it a social and community endeavor as well. I've developed six peer inquiry practices that you can do with a partner, face-to-face or remotely. Each peer inquiry practice is its own individual set of questions designed to help you access your true Self and speak from Self-leadership to another person. You can do one at a time or go through all six peer inquiry practices in a row.

As you begin each peer inquiry practice, decide who will ask first and who will respond first. The person asking will read the first question, wait for a response, then read the second question, wait for a response, and so on, until their partner has responded to the last question. Then switch roles.

Here are pointers for the process:

• Understand the words of the inquiry.

- Unhook awareness from thinking and allow awareness to look back and know directly with awareness.

- From this new awareness-based knowing, let words arise and speak them without going to thinking.

- It is not so important what your answer is but that you look with awareness and learn to speak and relate to another person from awareness-based knowing.

GLIMPSE **Peer Inquiry Practice 1**

1. Who is hearing?

2. Where is the hearer?

3. What is here if there is no problem to solve now? ■

GLIMPSE **Peer Inquiry Practice 2**

1. Tell me about what is aware without going to thought.

2. Tell me about that which is aware, which is beyond words.

3. What is aware of the six senses?

4. Does this awareness have a color, shape, or location?

5. What is it like if awareness knows the six senses from within? ■

GLIMPSE **Peer Inquiry Practice 3**

1. When awareness drops below the neck and opens, what does this open-hearted awareness know?

2. What does the welcoming heart know?

3. Is this awake awareness an experience occurring to you, or is this who you are?

4. What is the relationship between awareness and any unpleasant feelings?

5. What is the relationship between awareness and beliefs and stories?

6. What is the relationship between awareness and the fear of the fear of death? ■

GLIMPSE **Peer Inquiry Practice 4**

1. What is aware of movement and mental sensations?

2. Where is the "I"?

3. Is there anything missing or anything that needs to be pushed away?

4. Can you live from open-hearted awareness? ■

GLIMPSE **Peer Inquiry Practice 5**

1. What is here before the "I" thought arises?

2. Is this awake awareness an experience,
   or is it me? Is it what is?

3. What does open-hearted awareness know? ■

GLIMPSE **Peer Inquiry Practice 6**

1. Who is hearing?

2. Where is the hearer?

3. Where are we hearing from?

4. What is here, now, when there
   is no problem to solve?

5. Where are you aware from?

6. Tell me about the awareness that is knowing.

7. What does everything feel like
   as awareness-energy?

8. What do you know from your heart? ■

These peer inquiries can help make the transition from a passive stage of resting as awake awareness to rewiring, talking, and walking from open-hearted awareness. This can also build community. When you finish the series with each other, continue to talk about other things in your life from this new awareness-based way of knowing and relating. The goal is for us all to awaken together and help others from our natural compassionate motivation.

9

Glimpsing All the Way Home

I hope you are enjoying this journey of effortless mindfulness and have found some helpful mindful glimpses to discover a true taste of freedom. I also hope you will continue in the way of effortless mindfulness in your daily life. Waking up and growing up both need consistency to change the old habits of consciousness to a new normal. However, consistency is not easy. As you know from other helpful habits that need regular practice, like exercising, eating vegetables, drinking water, and brushing your teeth, the main support of effortless mindfulness is consistency—small glimpses, many times during the day.

You may have noticed the everyday chattering mind starts to establish its habit of creating a small self or "mini-me" first thing in the morning. So a morning meditation is important to transition from sleep to wakeful living. You might enjoy this unique suggestion, which is to do a mindful glimpse in the morning while still in bed. When you wake up in bed, hit the snooze alarm and roll over on your back. Then you can use your smartphone (with earphones if you're not alone) or do a mindful glimpse from memory as a transition from dream/sleep to "waking up" in both senses of the phrase.

Alternatively, begin by getting out of bed and finding a place to sit with your eyes open or closed for your morning mindful glimpse. Start your meditation session with a way of settling in and calming your animal body and brain that works for you. This is where many people find deliberate mindfulness practice to be especially helpful. A breath practice, chanting, prayer, chi gong, yoga, lovingkindness, checking in with your inner parts, dedicating your practice to all beings, and/or connecting to your supports can be helpful before a mindful glimpse.

Tune in, marinate, and entrain your brain to begin the day from effortless mindfulness as best you can. This first fine-tuning of your operating system is important. The main shift is moving from *looking to thoughts* to *looking to awareness*, which looks to itself. Then awake awareness can include thoughts, feelings, and energy arising as effortless mindfulness embodied.

You can set an alert in the calendar on your smartphone to remind you to do mindful glimpses throughout the day. You can record the mindful glimpses in your own voice or listen to one of my recordings. It is particularly helpful to learn to do the mindful glimpses with eyes open, such as while looking out the window, walking, or looking over your computer screen, and you can then return to your daily activities from effortless heart-mindfulness.

Here is a simple guide to use as a reference to learn how to do small glimpses anytime during the day:

REMEMBERING TO REMEMBER

1. *Recognize* that you are caught, attached, or identified.

2. *Realize* there is another way to be.

3. *Remember* a glimpse method of returning or re-recognizing that has worked for you.

4. *Unhook local awareness* by unblending with thinking or a part. Let awareness turn around to spacious awareness or move down within the body.

5. *Shift* into already awake awareness.

6. *Feel* awareness aware of itself.

7. *See* the dance between formlessness and form from awareness-energy.

8. *Know* from embodied open-hearted awareness.

9. *Let be* by resting as the Ground of Being without thinking to be or doing to be. Marinate and mix awake awareness and aliveness. Invite all parts, thoughts, and emotions into the boundless Heart and tender human heart.

10. *Remain undistracted* without effort.

11. *Do from Being* by beginning to rewire your brain and ego functioning, to operate from open-hearted awareness and Self-leadership.

12. *Detox, welcome, and liberate* by allowing open-hearted awareness to welcome exiled parts and unburden protective parts.

13. *When you notice you've become re-identified,* simply say, "No big surprise, just re-recognize."

14. Then, with small glimpses, *learn to return, and train to remain.*

Your experiences doing the mindful glimpses are meant to be the most important takeaways from this practice book. Not even the best writing or most precise intellectual understanding can replace your intimate experience of these shifts of awareness. Using these mindful glimpses, I hope you are able to get a taste of the unconditional love that you truly are. I hope you will keep this book close as a guide and support for your journey of compassionate awakening.

Small awakenings may come from glimpses, surrendering, marinating, or spontaneous moments that we can't foresee. The premise of mindful glimpses is that the peace and love we seek is already here, and it can be intentionally and immediately discovered. We do not have to wait for luck or grace because grace is already here, even though it may feel hidden. The paradoxical truth is that there is always awakeness and always unfolding. There is nothing to do to be the awake awareness that you already are, but there is the unfolding relationship and intimate dance of the formless and form.

We start out with the normal way we've all mostly been walking around: as the small self, with the small thinking mind doing its best to care for itself, using attention to witness its pain, to embrace its circumstances, but also getting overwhelmed and still perceiving itself as small and separate.

We've now learned pointers that can lead us into immediate awakenings, that open us out of what the thinker "thought" reality was and into a new view and new you. These "aha!" moments (that are sometimes "ha-ha!" moments) may last a few seconds or may move us from a meditation state to a new stage of life. The unfolding of our awakening often includes difficulties as we stumble our way toward living from open-hearted awareness. Awakening does not add or change anything ultimately. It is a shift of the background already-stable awake awareness to become the ground of our seeing and being. Awakening shifts us out of our limited view that does not see awakeness and into a loving, interconnected, joyful flow of life.

When we have seen through the constructs of who we thought we were, the most constant experience that remains is love, in its multiple forms: gratitude, patience, acceptance, compassion, joy, beauty, and bliss. We are experiencing all of life from open-hearted awareness. We find ourselves so effortlessly loving, and we know ourselves as fully lovable. And more: we know ourselves as love itself.

As we live life, it doesn't mean it will always be easy. Pain, loss, and difficulties are a natural part of everyone's life, yet we can discover the support of effortless mindfulness to open us to interconnection with all of life. We are all on the same journey and part of the same human family. I admire and join you in continuing to wake up and grow up for the sake of all beings. I have found that the shift from head to heart leads to compassionate activity and commitment to social justice. We can develop a sense of courage and community and find the well-being and love that are within us and unite us all as we honor and thank the beautiful mystery.

Appendix

Traps, Detours, and Rerouting Instructions

It is always helpful to have a map when we go on a journey, or even better, a GPS system. Even if the voice in the GPS is a little mechanical, it can be useful in those moments when we get off course and it magically says, "Rerouting," and then gives us updated directions.

Some of the most important instructions available from ancient wisdom traditions and contemporary psychology include pointers regarding the potential ways people can get stuck, sidetracked, lost, or confused on their journey home. Below are some of the most common traps and detours that I have noticed in working with thousands of students.

SPACED OUT

Once you unhook local awareness from thought and open to space, you will feel some relief and freedom from the chattering mind. This is a crucial step, but space is not the final frontier. We do not want to remain as a detached mindful witness or in disembodied pure awareness. While the first step is to discover that space is free of mental obsession, the next step is to discover that space is not absence, but space itself is aware. We can then also discover that spacious awareness is inherently within our body.

BLISSED IN

When you unhook local awareness and drop down below the neck, you will experience your subtle body as a return to your senses. This can be a pleasant state and is often experienced through practices like calm abiding, chanting, mantra, dancing, music, massage, exercise, or drugs. If you get stuck here, however, you can become a "bliss ninny" or be only "hippy-happy." While this experience of the subtle body, or inner body presence, is free of the mind, it is still bound by our skin and subtle energy body. The subtle body experience is not yet open to spacious awareness, nor to the experience of interconnection with others.

STUCK IN STILLNESS

When local awareness unhooks from the mind and discovers inner stillness in the body, we can fall back to sleep into the pleasant effects of the luscious stillness. This experience, often discovered through long periods of sitting meditation, can be a detour because it has stillness but does not have movement or awareness.

THE WITNESS PROTECTION PROGRAM

We can get caught in the initial stage of mindful observer or witnessing from spacious awareness and try to live from the meditative tower or the spacious sky, disconnected from the ocean of emotion. Once we are aware from spacious awareness that we are free of identification with the small self, it is still possible to land in a new dualistic view that is detached from both our body and the interconnectedness with all things. This mindful witness is a key step of transcendence, but it is not the end goal. If we live as the detached witness, we will be free of threat, but we will miss community and the juiciness of life. Instead, for a fully embodied experience of wholeness, we can continue on our journey by returning from spacious awareness back to the boundless aliveness of open-hearted awareness.

GETTING BORED BACK TO THE MIND

As we stabilize in a greater level of well-being, we will need to get used to feeling peace of mind. The transition out of the frenetic activity of our mind at first may come as a relief but might at some point start to feel like a withdrawal from the level of excitement and drama we had been used to. In this gap of not-knowing, a part of us may feel that the peace we had been seeking feels unstimulating, dull, and boring. We might get "bored back to the mind," seeking more excitement. Instead, we can be encouraged to wait in this lull for the natural curiosity, joy, and new knowing to appear from this place of peace. Eventually, a different kind of excitement arises, like the way a kid feels on the first day of summer vacation. If we get bored back to the mind, we can notice the part of us that is bored and learn to listen to it and welcome it from open-hearted awareness.

GETTING SCARED BACK TO THE MIND

The everyday mind has been our primary way of orienting ourselves for identity and safety. The small self that is created within the everyday mind operates like a computer that has been programmed to follow certain rules. Thought-free awake awareness is not included on the list of the everyday mind's approved programs. The everyday mind's safety programs instead have rules like "Orient by thought" and "Avoid the void," which may send the alerting program of the ego defenses into a panic. So when we shift out of everyday mind, the ego defense program reacts as if it were protecting us from death, but it is protecting a limited thought pattern! The confusion happens because the small self sends adrenaline into the body and creates a feeling of fear and danger as if there were a physical threat to the system. There is no real danger if you can shift into awake awareness as the new operating system. There still may be a car alarm going off, but there is no thief to be found. The feeling of fear is real, but the reason for it is not.

If you get scared back to the mind, you can begin to glimpse again. As you do, you'll learn to feel the fear and embrace the fear from awake awareness. There will be a period of adjustment and growth that includes some disorientation before reorientation.

GOING BACK TO THE MIND FOR A SECOND OPINION

Once we have experienced awake awareness, and before we are rewired to open-hearted awareness, we can get drawn back to the small mind to try to know whether or not we're doing it right. The small mind is not capable of knowing about the fresh territory of awake awareness, but it *will* be glad to give an opinion like, "This is ridiculous," or "I don't think I'm getting it, but everyone else seems to be," or "I might as well give up, I'm never going to get this," or the subtler, "Yes, but . . ." The small mind is actually right, as it will never get this—because the small mind can't—but you already *are* this awake awareness, which is the source of mind. The solution begins when we know from nonconceptual awake awareness.

ATTENTION OVERLOAD: "PAYING" ATTENTION UNTIL YOU BECOME BANKRUPT

The main reason many people cannot focus is not attention deficit disorder but what I call *attention overload disorder*. You can use attention to develop the skills of concentration and calm focus, but you can easily overexert yourself into attention overload if you stop development at this stage of trying to concentrate from small mind. Attention has the ability to be precise but can also be dry and miserly. Attention is not the form of awareness used to recognize awake awareness. You must continue to discover awake awareness and effortless mindfulness within the interconnected field of open-hearted awareness.

The key transition from using attention to using local awareness is to have local awareness step out of the thought-based, ego-centered small mind. If local awareness has not unhooked or detached from thought, you will be trying to be mindful from the everyday mind by using attention, which will keep you from knowing awake awareness. The point here is to stress that attention overload happens when you use attention as the only form of awareness. Many people who have been diagnosed with attention deficit disorder (ADD) have been helped by effortless mindfulness. You will get a feel for the distinct difference between attention concentrating from small mind and the relief of local awareness focusing from awake awareness.

GOLDILOCKS: PORRIDGE TOO COLD, PORRIDGE TOO HOT

As I mentioned earlier using my colleague Anna-Lisa Adelberg's metaphor, if you're too far back into awake awareness or conceptual mind, then people experience you as "porridge too cold." If you are too much in subtle body awareness or emotionally enmeshed with your own parts or with other people's feelings, then people experience you as "porridge too hot." If you are relating and creating from effortless heart-mindfulness and Self-leadership, people will exclaim, "Porridge just right!"

SCARECROW AWAKENING

This one is the first in a series of *The Wizard of Oz* metaphors. In this type of scarecrow awakening, we try to awaken through reading a lot of spiritual books or understanding who we are through intellectual concepts. Our conceptual mind is about as useful as a head filled with straw when it comes to knowing awake awareness as our true nature. We need to shift into an awake awareness–based knowing.

TIN MAN AWAKENING

Here we have a strong experience of emptiness and no-self, but there is not enough heart yet. Here we've awakened from mind, body, and emotion but not yet into open-hearted awareness. Keep following the yellow brick road!

COWARDLY LION AWAKENING

In this one, we're learning to go beyond the doer, opening to a new vulnerability, a new avenue for action to come through. But we can get stuck with not yet having developed the courage of open-hearted awareness to be and do in the world. People at this stage sometimes become aggressive or have a know-it-all persona, like the Cowardly Lion pompously chasing Toto, but that action is coming from defensiveness, pride, or fear. Many people have reported the big shift in doing social justice work from the motivation of love and compassion, rather than fear and anger.

DOROTHY AWAKENING

Here we get stuck in perpetual seeking, going around and around on the yellow brick road, trying to get to freedom without realizing that we have been home all along.

TOTO AWAKENING

The trap here is feeling like you are only a small animal rather than experiencing your vast, interconnected Self. Try saying "total awakening" with a Castilian Spanish accent. (It sounds like a slight lisp to English-speaking ears.) Don't miss Toto awakening by thinking that anything is left out or separate. Does a dog, like Toto, have Buddha nature? Dog-Zen says yes. (Cow-Zen says mu.)

THE RUBY SLIPPERS OF EFFORTLESS MINDFULNESS

The trap here is getting discouraged and feeling lost and overwhelmed by the journey. Remember the good witch Glinda's advice about the ruby slippers: you've had the power to return home all along.

INTELLECTUALIZATION

My teacher Tulku Urgyen Rinpoche has said about realization of your true nature that "the great danger is when one just leaves it as intellectual understanding."[1] Awakening is grounded in experiencing nonconceptual awareness. Any fixed ideas or beliefs that we create about awakening, that we become fascinated with, can bring us back to a small self and small mind. Instead, we can choose to stay with the natural unfolding, which will lead us through the stage of not-knowing into a new spontaneous heart-knowing.

BEING UNDER THE INFLUENCE OF THE ULTIMATE

This is the feeling that the ultimate dimension is the only thing that is real and everything else is illusion. My understanding of nonduality is that on the ultimate level, appearances are unreal, but on the relative level, they are appearing. The relative is made of the ultimate like a wave is made of the ocean. Nonduality is not the exclusive domain of the ultimate reality. The relative is a precious expression of the ultimate. Our being is both transcendent and immanent.

ONENESS ONLY

When people are released from dualistic perception, they often describe the initial experience as "oneness." The experience of oneness can occur when there is a dropping of ego-identification, such as during a peak experience, where there is a feeling of "I am one with everything." The term *nondual* does not mean oneness. The Sanskrit word for nonduality, *advaita*, was used for a reason: it means "not two." The ancient mystics had other words for oneness that could have been used, but they chose *advaita*. *Nondual* means both/and, inseparable, all-at-once, and simultaneous: not one, not two, not several, not empty, but all of these.

SAUNA MEDITATION STATE

I call getting caught in a calm, relaxed, sleeplike state that is comfortably numb "sauna meditation." Tsoknyi Rinpoche refers to this as "stupid meditation."[2] The goal of meditation is not to stop thoughts or just be very relaxed. This can be an important first step to soothe the animal of our mind and body, but awakening is alert, interconnected, creative, and compassionate.

AVOIDING THE VOID

The small mind naturally fears the unknown. It spends time and energy projecting negative beliefs onto the emptiness of no thought and no action and defending against the void and egolessness. It fears losing control and dying. But as we transition out of small self, we discover that emptiness, space, and the unknown are the boundless ground of our being, which is safe and includes everything.

LOOKING BUT NOT LEAPING

Some people are fascinated with the ultimate but never go beyond meditation practices that develop the relative level. This can be more of a teacher problem than a student problem, as many students are eager to experience ultimate reality. It's helpful for students to have a map to know how to let go and what to go let go into. But eventually we have to go beyond everything we've been taught and discover our inner teachers. Truly knowing if we're in the right place can only be known by the new knowing that arises after you make the leap.

LOVING THE DESCRIPTION BUT NOT TAKING THE PRESCRIPTION

Many people love the beautiful words in books, poetry, and teachings but have not found the directions, prescriptions, courage, curiosity, beginner's mind, or commitment that are necessary for the journey. It is one thing to read the map and another to experience the territory.

SPIRITUAL BYPASS

In *Toward a Psychology of Awakening*, John Welwood points out this potential trap: "There is often a tendency to use spiritual practice to try to rise above our emotional and personal issues—all those messy, unresolved matters that weigh us down. I call this tendency to avoid or prematurely transcend basic human needs, feelings, and developmental tasks *spiritual bypassing*."[3]

PSYCHOLOGICAL UNDERPASS

Psychological underpass is the term I use to describe doing psychotherapy from an ego-identity, using only a bio-psycho-social map and tools. Important healing and personal growth can happen with conventional psychotherapy, but only to a certain level without discovering our true nature: no-self Self.

PARKING AT THE GRAND CANYON

This is like having an initial amazing, vast, opening experience of your true nature but then stopping partway on your journey and setting up camp.

NOTHING TO DO/DOING NOTHING

Because awake awareness is self-maintaining and self-liberating without "me" doing anything, we can believe that there is no need to take any action on any level. Although the small, initial effort of letting go, stopping, or surrendering leads us beyond the initial doer, in reality, awake awareness does have intention and the ability to create and relate from Self-leadership.

STOPPING AT NOT-KNOWING

Not-knowing is the transition between conceptual knowing and awake awareness. If you stop in "don't-know mind," which is the beginning stage of true knowing, then you are free of the old information processor in your head, but you have not yet rewired your system to hook up with awake awareness that is the new nonconceptual operating system. It is a relief when we step out of the small mind, but we can get stuck in a meditative gap of not-knowing, which can lead to a couch potato phase. Instead, we need to keep moving, first from mental knowing into not-knowing, then into nonconceptual awake awareness, then to a not-knowing that knows, and finally to open-hearted awareness.

NOBODY HOME

After the experience of ego-identification falls away, the opposite belief can replace it: "There is nobody here." Often people speaking from this view will say something like, "There is no one named Tom here, and I see there never was. I feel free, though my partner says I'm disconnected." This is a transitional phase and is experienced in such a way because we started from a strong experience of ego as "this is who I am," so when ego-identification drops away, it can feel as if no one is here anymore. In fact, the one you took yourself to be is no longer experienced and is no longer the experiencer. So there is a transition, or a gap, of no-self, but then awake awareness becomes embodied and open-hearted to be a more intimate human being. Our ego functions and personality will always be a part of us as an awake human being.

FUNDAMENTAL FUNDAMENTALISM

People fall into this trap if they take initial awakening as a philosophy that is either right or wrong. In this trap, awakening and its insights get co-opted by intellectual ideas. Awakening can be made into a spiritual experience that "I" am having, which either reinforces the ideas that this "I" had before or creates a new "right religion." Please don't become too rigid and serious or forget that "fun" cannot be taken out of our *fun*damental nature!

ETHICAL RELATIVITY

This is a detour that happens when people go beyond dualistic perception and say, "Everything is relative, an illusion, and the play of consciousness, so I can do whatever I want." This is a common and potentially dangerous trap after initial head awakening. The initial awakening out of categories of good and bad and the controlling superego leads to a freedom from the sense of internal and societal "shoulds." This can be greatly beneficial in that it releases us from binds that hold the false identity together. However, it is possible to stop at the "freedom from" small self stage without getting to the "freedom to" awake awareness stage. If we stop after head awakening, it can lead to a regression to an adolescent level of ethics and acting out on impulses related to sex, money, or power, as we've seen with some spiritual teachers. In this way, some people will take initial awakening as a free pass to do whatever they want because "everything is the play of the Divine."

SPIRITUAL ROBOT

The feeling of being not only disidentified but detached from all emotions and preferences can lead to the point where, when you are asked, "What type of tea would you like?" you respond, "All tea is the same." The goal is not to transcend emotions, desires, and preferences but to shift out of the suffering caused by ego-identification and into living from an interconnected, joyful, compassionate, and awake human life.

EARNING AWAKENING

When we think we have to earn awakening, we get caught in a kind of striving and seeking, as if awakening is something we have to be worthy of or that is dependent on effort, works, or skill. In some ways, the first awakening is the realization that we are already essentially awake.

STUCK IN THE STUDENT ROLE

If the role of a teacher is to introduce students to their own inner teacher, then the student's role is to meet their inner teacher. We might get stuck by projecting our inner teachers onto an outer teacher. Some students remain in the nest too long or remain in the dependent student role of following directions without embodying the teachings. Some students might idealize teachers and remain in a dependent role, doubting that they themselves can ever awaken. Other students are continually spirituality shopping and going to different teachers as a way of entertainment and avoidance of facing the meeting of repressed parts as necessary for spiritual growth.

ONE AND DONE

Some students have a belief that once they've had the initial experience of awakening from dualistic mind, they've arrived, and that they'll stay there, without going back to other ways of being they are more used to. Instead, a shift into embodied awakening requires time for unfolding and rewiring to be able to live from effortless heart-mindfulness.

NIHILISM OR ETERNALISM

Both of these are extremes. Nihilism is the view that because everything is empty, everything is meaningless. Eternalism is the view that there is a thing called "me" that will exist as it is forever. Being empty of a separate self means that we are interconnected to life. Remember, emptiness means interconnection.

TRYING TO KILL THE EGO THAT DOESN'T EXIST

This is a way of using aggression, will, effort, and control to try to get rid of or subdue the ego identity. However, the ego is not an entity that exists; it is a mental and emotional pattern. Fighting against the pattern reinforces its strength! Once we discover awake awareness as the foundation of who we are, ego functions can relax and semi-retire from trying to do a second job of ego identity.

AWAKENING AS ONE-STOP SHOPPING

Awakening does not mean that all of your human developmental areas will go to an elevated level immediately. For example, discovering the wisdom of open-hearted awareness does not mean you will immediately be able to win all Trivial Pursuit games, play concert piano, or have excellent communication skills with loved ones or people at work. In Zen, there is a saying: "Enlightenment is acceptance of imperfection." We need to continue to both wake up and grow up.

WHITEWASHING OR WEARING ROSE-COLORED GLASSES

When we do this, we are acting as if the relative world is "rosy," or we are allowing ourselves to be blind to human suffering. This distancing comes from false beliefs that awakening means that we will never have any problems and that we will be able to escape from the human condition. Instead, we are able to experience both pleasant and unpleasant feelings and respond more courageously to inner and outer pain.

PSYCHIC DIMENSION DETOUR

It is not unusual to reach a stage of awakening in which you become extremely sensitive, on a subtle or psychic level of perception, to other people's emotional states or subtle aspects of your surrounding environment. This perceptual opening or overload will usually calm down on its own after a while, but it can be helpful to get feedback from others who have experienced this to realize that though you're "out of your (small) mind," you haven't gone crazy!

There are two traps here: First, you might become fascinated with these psychic perceptions or powers, which are not necessary for awakening, and let them sidetrack you via distraction and dispersed attention. Second, you might get scared or overwhelmed because the new feelings or perceptions are unknown or intense, and you start to shut down. It can all feel like too much information. The way through is to open up to the awake awareness dimension inside and all around so that you can remain sensitive while allowing the intelligence of awake awareness to integrate all of the input, new sensitivity, and experiences without overwhelm.

CONEY ISLAND HOT DOG OF SPIRITUAL PRIDE

We may have the belief that the ego identity will wake up or that the person "me" is awake. Arrogance or pride can show up in the spiritual path with thoughts or beliefs of specialness such as, "I am one with everything, but others are not," or "I am an awake butterfly, and others are asleep caterpillars." In truth, I am unique like everyone else, and awakeness is equally within each of us, as each of us, whether we know it or not. Buddha supposedly said upon realization, "I and all beings have awakened."

SPIRITUAL SUPEREGO

This is a harsh inner critic, an aspect of the ego-self that remains dominant and subtly drives you to renunciation, self-denial, or judgment of yourself or others around "spiritual" beliefs, ideas, or right and wrong actions. This is a protective part that is trying to help, and it is best met with listening and love rather than *judging the judger*.

RUBBER BAND EFFECT, OR GETTING IT/LOSING IT

This can be a typical experience during the initial stage of having glimpses of awakening. The inertia of our habits of mind has a power that draws us back to the magnetic ego-center. While our awakening path unfolds, as long as the unconditioned spacious awareness remains the only alternative to ego-identity, then we will have to come back to the ego in order to function. Since we can't live as a human being while remaining in pure awake awareness only, we'll experience "losing it" and having to return to ego identity in order to function, until form and formlessness are discovered to not be separate.

Acknowledgments

So many people have touched my life and influenced me in ways that I can never fully express. I am so grateful for each breath in my precious human life. I want to thank all the people I have come in contact with, especially students and clients, who have given me more than they can imagine.

I'd like to thank my three amazing primary editors, Alice Peck, Olivia Frazao, and Elah Schild, for their tremendous help and support. I also want to acknowledge my consulting editor, Kelly Notaras, as well as Jennifer Brown and the amazing team at Sounds True.

To my colleagues and fellow teachers Scott McBride, Anna-Lisa Adelberg, Adyashanti, Richard Schwartz, Father Thomas Keating, Chad Cascarilla, Tara Brach, Shinzen Young, Richard Miller, Anam Thubten, Lama Surya Das, Stephan Bodian, Mirabai Starr, Kurt Johnson, Daniel Siegel, and my cat Duffy.

To my teachers, whose guidance and open-hearted discussions have nourished me and brought me great joy: Godwin Samararatne, Dhammasiri, Khenchen Thrangu Rinpoche, Dzogchen Ponlop Rinpoche, Chogyal Namkhai Norbu, Traleg Rinpoche, Daniel Brown, Hameed Ali, Anam Thubten, Mingyur Rinpoche, and Tsoknyi Rinpoche.

To my board members and team at the Open-Hearted Awareness Institute. I am not able to thank everyone who has helped me by name, but know that your support has helped this book become available to many people.

To all my family and friends, especially my loving wife, Paige, who have supported me through the writing of this book and beyond.

Notes

CHAPTER 1

1. Mihaly Csikszentmihalyi, "Flow, the Secret to Happiness," February 2004, TED video, 18:56, ted.com/talks/ mihaly_csikszentmihalyi_on_flow?language=en.

CHAPTER 2

1. Tulku Urgyen Rinpoche, *Rainbow Painting: A Collection of Miscellaneous Aspects of Development and Completion*, trans. Erik Pema Kunsang (Hong Kong: Ranjung Yeshe Publications, 1995), 110.
2. Tulku Urgyen Rinpoche, "The Kind of Guru I Had," Lion's Roar: Buddhist Wisdom for Our Time, September 1, 2005, lionsroar.com/the-kind-of-guru-i-had/.
3. Jon Kabat-Zinn, *Wherever You Go, There You Are: Mindfulness Meditation in Everyday Life* (New York: Hachette Books, 2005), 4.
4. *Merriam-Webster*, s.v. "attention," accessed August 22, 2018, merriam-webster.com/dictionary/attention.
5. William James, *The Principles of Psychology*, vol. 1 (Massachusetts: Peter Smith Pub Inc, 1979), 176.
6. Zoran Josipovic et al., "Influence of Meditation on Anti-Correlated Networks in the Brain," *Frontiers in Human Neuroscience* 5 (January 2011): 183, doi.org/10.3389/fnhum.2011.00183.
7. Zoran Josipovic, "Freedom of the Mind," *Frontiers in Psychology* 4 (August 2013): 538, doi.org/10.3389/fpsyg.2013.00538.
8. Poppy L.A. Schoenberg et al., "Mapping Complex Mind States: EEG Neural Substrates of Meditative Unified Compassionate Awareness," *Consciousness and Cognition* 57 (January 2018): 41–53, doi.org/10.1016/j.concog.2017.11.003.
9. Schoenberg, "Mapping Complex Mind States," 43.

CHAPTER 3

1. Dzogchen Ponlop Rinpoche, *Wild Awakening: The Heart of Mahamudra and Dzogchen* (Boston: Shambhala Publications, 2003), 30–31.

2. Andrew Olendzki, "The Fourth Foundation of Mindfulness," *Insight Journal*, Barre Center for Buddhist Studies, Spring 2004, buddhistinquiry.org/article/the-fourth-foundation-of-mindfulness/.

3. Thich Nhat Hanh, *Interbeing* (Berkeley: Parallax Press, 1987), 4.

CHAPTER 5

1. *Merriam-Webster*, s.v. "attention," accessed August 22, 2018, merriam-webster.com/dictionary/attention.

2. Daniel J. Siegel, *The Mindful Brain: Reflection and Attunement in the Cultivation of Well-Being* (New York: WW Norton & Company, 2007).

3. Adyashanti, *The Most Important Thing: Discovering Truth at the Heart of Life* (Boulder, CO: Sounds True, 2019), 113.

CHAPTER 6

1. "Cortical/Cerebral Visual Impairment, Traumatic Brain Injury, and Neurological Vision Loss," American Foundation for the Blind, accessed August 5, 2018, afb.org/info/living-with-vision-loss/eye-conditions/cortical-visual-impairment-traumatic- brain-injury-and-neurological-vision-loss/123.

2. Ken McLeod, *An Arrow to the Heart: A Commentary on the Heart Sutra* (Bloomington, IN: Trafford, 2007), 2.

3. Ken McLeod, *Wake Up to Your Life: Discovering the Buddhist Path of Attention* (San Francisco: Harper, 2001), 223.

CHAPTER 7

1. Richard Schwartz, *Internal Family Systems Therapy* (New York: Guilford Press, 1997), 82.
2. Daniel J. Siegel, *The Developing Mind: How Relationships and the Brain Interact to Shape Who We Are*, 2nd ed. (New York: Guilford Press, 2015), 199.
3. Schwartz, *Internal Family Systems Therapy*, 106.

APPENDIX

1. "Tulku Urgyen Rinpoche—Interview for *Vajradhatu Sun*, 1985," We Are Perfect Buddha Mind (blog), translated by Erik Pema Kunsang, October 29, 2009, wearebuddhamind.blogspot. com/2009/10/tulku-urgyen-rinpoche-interview-for.html.
2. Tsoknyi Rinpoche, "A Very Human Condition (Part 2 of 2)," Pundarika Foundation, accessed October 7, 2018, tsoknyirinpoche. org/1439/a-very-human-condition-part-two-of-two/.
3. John Welwood, *Toward a Psychology of Awakening: Buddhism, Psychotherapy, and the Path of Personal and Spiritual Transformation* (Boston: Shambhala Publications, 2000), 12.

List of Mindful Glimpses

Index

About the Author

Loch Kelly, MDiv, LCSW, is author of *Shift into Freedom: The Science and Practice of Open-Hearted Awareness*, which was named one of the "Top 10 Best Books of the Year" by *Spirituality & Health* magazine. He is an educator, licensed psychotherapist, and recognized leader in the field of meditation affiliated with Adyashanti. Loch is the founder of the nonprofit Open-Hearted Awareness Institute. He is a graduate of Columbia University and Union Theological Seminary, where he received a fellowship to study Insight Meditation, Advaita, and Tibetan Buddhism in Sri Lanka, India, and Nepal. He has worked in community mental health, established homeless shelters, and counseled family members of 9/11 victims in New York City.

Loch trained with Tulku Urgyen Rinpoche and served on the Teacher's Council at New York Insight Meditation Center. He offers the advanced yet simple direct methods of effortless mindfulness informed by psychology and social engagement. He collaborates with neuroscientists at Yale University, the University of Pennsylvania, and New York University to study how awareness training can enhance compassion and well-being.

For more information, visit Loch's website, effortlessmindfulness. org, which has a list of his upcoming retreats and workshops and free audio mindful glimpses. Loch's YouTube channel also has free videos of his teachings and practices.

About Sounds True

Sounds True is a multimedia publisher whose mission is to inspire and support personal transformation and spiritual awakening. Founded in 1985 and located in Boulder, Colorado, we work with many of the leading spiritual teachers, thinkers, healers, and visionary artists of our time. We strive with every title to preserve the essential "living wisdom" of the author or artist. It is our goal to create products that not only provide information to a reader or listener, but that also embody the quality of a wisdom transmission.

For those seeking genuine transformation, Sounds True is your trusted partner. At SoundsTrue.com you will find a wealth of free resources to support your journey, including exclusive weekly audio interviews, free downloads, interactive learning tools, and other special savings on all our titles.

To learn more, please visit SoundsTrue.com/freegifts or call us toll-free at 800.333.9185.

sounds true
WAKING UP THE WORLD